Scotland's Unsolved Mysteries
of the Twentieth Century

RICHARD WILSON

ROBERT HALE · LONDON

© *Richard Wilson 1989*
First published in Great Britain 1989

Robert Hale Limited
Clerkenwell House
Clerkenwell Green
London EC1R 0HT

British Library Cataloguing in Publication Data

Wilson, Richard
  Scotland's unsolved mysteries of the twentieth
  century.
  1. Scotland. Mysteries. History
  I. Title
  001.9'4'09411I

  ISBN 0–7090–3828–3

Photoset in Palatino by
Derek Doyle & Associates, Mold, Clwyd.
Printed in Great Britain by
St Edmundsbury Press Ltd, Bury St Edmunds, Suffolk.
Bound by WBC Bookbinders Limited.

Scotland's Unsolved Mysteries
of the Twentieth Century

The son of a Scottish police detective, Richard Wilson has worked as a journalist in Fleet Street, Holland, Belgium and Scotland. He edited *The Scotsman Magazine* throughout its nine-year existence and is now a freelance editor living in Edinburgh with his wife Alison and their two children. He is the author of two acclaimed thrillers, *The Amsterdam Silver* and *The Press Gang*.

Contents

For Charlotte, Harry, and Chris

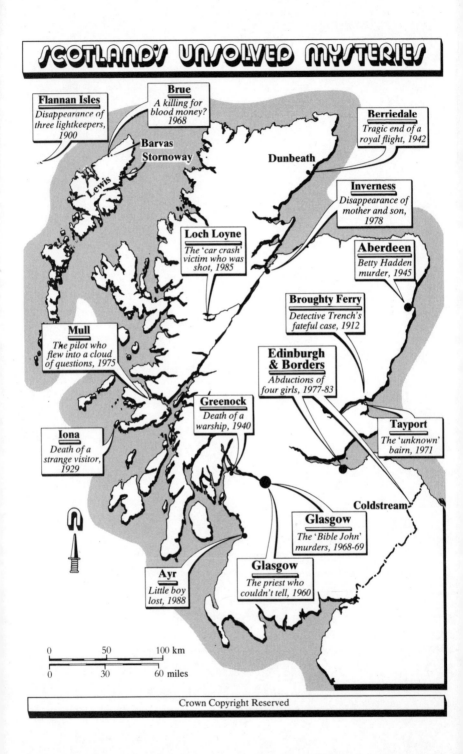

SCOTLAND'S UNSOLVED MYSTERIES

Flannan Isles
Disappearance of three lightkeepers, 1900

Brue
A killing for blood money? 1968

Berriedale
Tragic end of a royal flight, 1942

Barvas
Stornoway

Lewis

Dunbeath

Inverness
Disappearance of mother and son, 1978

Loch Loyne
The 'car crash' victim who was shot, 1985

Aberdeen
Betty Hadden murder, 1945

Broughty Ferry
Detective Trench's fateful case, 1912

Mull
The pilot who flew into a cloud of questions, 1975

Edinburgh & Borders
Abductions of four girls, 1977-83

Greenock
Death of a warship, 1940

Tayport
The 'unknown' bairn, 1971

Iona
Death of a strange visitor, 1929

Coldstream

Glasgow
The 'Bible John' murders, 1968-69

Ayr
Little boy lost, 1988

Glasgow
The priest who couldn't tell, 1960

| 0 | 50 | 100 km |
| 0 | 30 | 60 miles |

Introduction

When my father was a police detective in a small Scottish coastal town, where rural serenity was always delightfully near at hand, it seemed as strange to me then as it does now, that he should have come home with spine-tingling tales of human malevolence that should not have fallen upon such young ears as mine. That where there are beaches and rivers, gaggling geese and silver salmon, there can also be sinister intent and sudden death that can equal anything a city has to offer.

And in Scotland, the cities have long boasted more than their fair share of murder and mayhem – a fact that I have acknowledged in this collection of modern mysteries, with several stories of urban murder in which the most perplexing element is the simple question: who did it and why?

The classic crimes of the cities have often been written about in volumes that have reached well back into previous centuries. Yet, within living memory and outwith the cities, there have been many mysterious incidents which now demand to be drawn together into one collection. So when the publisher asked me to look at this century's mysteries across the whole of Scotland, it was an invitation I could not resist, fascinated as I am by the fact that environmental factors seem to have little effect on criminal intent; and concerned as I am to know the full stories behind incidents that people still talk about in the shorthand of legend.

Did I say 'full stories'? Well, yes, I would *like* to know

9

them but unfortunately do not. As all the tales in this book remain mysteries, despite my optimistic efforts to get to the bottom of a few of them, I hope they are no less intriguing for that. In each case, I have tried to pull together all the known facts and I leave it to you, the reader, to come up with the solutions. And if you should know something that the rest of us don't, let me quote the words of a senior policeman involved in one of the country's most serious abduction cases: 'I am certain there is someone somewhere who ... had grave suspicions about a father, a son, a brother, or some like person and failed to report these to the police. Those suspicions must remain and I would urge that person to come forward, even at this late stage.'

1   The Unkept Light, 1900

Though three men dwell on Flannan Isle
To keep the lamp alight,
As we steered under the lee we caught
No glimmer through the night.

A passing ship at dawn had brought
The news, and quickly we set sail,
To find out what strange thing might ail
The keepers of the deep-sea light.

Wilfrid Wilson Gibson

The first person to notice something was wrong was the lookout on the passing tramp steamer *Archtor*, from Philadelphia. Reasonably certain of his ship's position just before midnight on 15 December 1900, he peered through the sea-fog expecting to see the two brilliant short flashes every thirty seconds that came from the Flannan Light. Normally they could be seen from a distance of twenty-four miles, and his ship was less than six miles away. But try as he might, he could not see the slightest flicker. All remained ominously dark and, although he did not then realize the significance of what he was reporting to his captain, that vaguely worrying revelation was to mark the beginning of one of the sea's most enduring mysteries.

Neither did the crew of the *Archtor*, steaming in such proximity to the remote lighthouse, realize just how near they were to solving the mystery there and then. For it was later established that whatever happened on that storm-beaten rocky islet, happened earlier that day. Had their curiousity been sufficiently aroused, they might have drawn closer, might even have attempted a landing, and might have discovered the true facts behind the riddle of the unkept light. In the absence of any immediate eye-witness evidence, however, the mystery has since given rise to much fantastic theorizing and confounded not only succeeding generations of experts but also the thousands of ordinary people all over the world who have been intrigued by Wilfrid Wilson Gibson's epic poem on the tragic affair, written – largely from the imagination – twelve years after it happened.

What happened? That has always been, and remains, the question. The mystery is on a par with that of the *Marie Celeste* and bears a shadowy resemblance to it; for the three keepers who should have been tending the light on Eilean Mor – one of the larger of the seven Flannan Islands, eighteen miles north-west of the Outer Hebridean island of Lewis – simply vanished, leaving only the most minimal of clues to their fate. They could not have left by boat, for they did not have one. And when crew of the relief tender *Hesperus* arrived there some eleven days later, the first man ashore found only, in the words of the poem, 'a door ajar and an untouched meal and an overtoppled chair'.

It was an unmitigated shock to them, for – having left Oban just before the *Archtor* men put in there to report their non-sighting of the light – the *Hesperus* crew had been unaware, as they battled through a fierce gale towards the far-off archipelago, that there was anything amiss at all. As far as they were concerned, this was just a normal relief operation. But when they finally came within sight of the stubby 75-feet-tall tower, standing 330 feet high on the topmost point of Eilean Mor, the absence of the usual welcoming flag was the first indication that all was not well. It was about noon on Boxing Day. The ship's captain, James Harvie, ordered that the steam whistle and siren be blasted twice, but there was no response from the blank windows. And a rocket fired from the ship, still so much under the weather that it could not safely release a landing boat, also died without an answer. With mounting alarm, Captain Harvie adjusted his telescope to scan the lighthouse anxiously ... its squat outbuilding ... the deserted plateau of the island ... then the long stone stairway which connected these, down an almost sheer cliffside, to the crashing spray of the sea. With the exception of fluttering sea-birds, he saw absolutely no sign of life. 'Something's wrong!' he shouted, then ordered the boat out despite the bad weather.

As the sea heaved and buffeted the tiny vessel against the western landing-stage, the relieving keeper, Joseph Moore, eventually managed to jump ashore to investigate. Clearly a brave man, he was nevertheless to be extremely traumatized by what he was yet to experience on the island ... so much so that his superintendent, Robert Muirhead, would later write that 'if this nervousness does not leave Moore, he will require to be transferred'.

As he climbed the awesome, snakelike flight of 160 steps up the 200-foot cliffside, Moore called out the names of the colleagues he hoped to find at the top, James Ducat, Thomas Marshall, and Donald McArthur, but all he received in reply were the shrieking cries of wheeling gulls and petrels. 'I went up and, on coming to the entrance gate,' he later wrote, 'I found it closed. I made for the door leading to the kitchen and storeroom. I found it closed. The door inside that was also closed but the kitchen door itself was open.'

When he went into the kitchen, Moore was surprised to find the table set as if a meal were about to begin. Apart from the overtoppled chair, everything seemed relatively normal, though the room had obviously been deserted for ... how long? The clocks had stopped. 'I looked at the fireplace and saw that the fire was not lighted for some days. I entered the rooms in succession and found the beds empty, just as they left them in the early morning. I did not take time to search further, for I naturally well knew that something serious had occurred. I darted outside and made for the landing ...'

There, he dramatically announced his fears to the waiting boatmen and persuaded two of them to join him in a more thorough investigation. They went back up with him to discover that 'unfortunately, my first impression was only too true'. Everything was in good order. Blinds were on the windows, pots and pans had been cleaned, the kitchen tidied up; and, on the professional side, the lamp had been trimmed, the oil fountains and canteens had been filled up, and the lens and machinery cleaned. It all seemed surprisingly correct, apart from the baffling fact that the keepers were not there.

Bewildered as he was, Moore still had a job to do. Once he had reported back to the *Hesperus*, he was given the help of two other seamen to man the light – and they soon had it back to work. 'We proceeded up to the light room and lighted the light at the proper time that night, and every night since.' That done, over the next two days, they continued the search for the missing men but, despite 'traversing the island from end to end, there was still nothing to convince us how it happened'.

Meanwhile, the *Hesperus* had made haste to Lewis to wire the news of the disaster to the Secretary of the Northern Lighthouse Board. And at 8.45 on that first night, an unhappily-disturbed Mr William Murdoch opened the door of his villa in a gaslit street in Trinity, Edinburgh, to receive the following message from a telegram boy:

A dreadful accident has happened at Flannans. The three keepers, Ducat, Marshall and the Occasional, have disappeared from the island. On our arrival there this afternoon no sign of life was to be seen on the island. Fired rocket, but, as no response was made, managed to land Moore who went up to the station but found no keepers there. The clocks were stopped and other signs indicated that the accident must have happened about a week ago. Poor fellows, they must have been blown over the cliffs or drowned trying to secure a crane or something like that.

Night coming on, we could not wait to make further investigation, but will go off again tomorrow morning to try and learn something as to their fate. I have left Moore, MacDonald, buoymaster, and two seamen on the island to keep the light burning until you make other arrangements. Will not return to Oban until I hear from you. I have repeated this wire to Muirhead, in case you are not at home. I will remain at the telegraph office tonight until it closes, if you wish to wire me. Master, Hesperus.

Captain Harvie's instant speculation on the cause of the lightkeepers' disappearance has to take its place among a plethora of ideas put forward over the years to explain the tragedy, and prominent among these has to be Superintendent Muirhead's. He was not only the last man to visit the lightkeepers alive, but also went to the island to investigate the tragedy a few days after its discovery.

But to appreciate the various theories, one has to understand the shape and topography of Eilean Mor. It is like a dog's head with the mouth on the right. The lighthouse is located in its eye socket, the east landing is under its chin, and the west landing up a high-sided, wave-lashed creek where a collar would be. A 400-yard incline rises from the west landing to the light.

In his report on the matter to the Commissioners of the Northern Lighthouses in Edinburgh, Superintendent Muirhead pointed out that the last entry on 'the slate' (where notes were chalked before logging) had been made by Mr Ducat, the principal keeper, on the morning of 15 December; and as the *Archtor* had not seen the light that evening, it could be assumed that the men had disappeared between the last entry on the slate and the time they should have ignited the light that afternoon. The *Archtor* had also reported 'a very heavy sea' in the area later that day. Muirhead therefore focused on the possibilities of the men being washed or blown away while working together on an emergency either outside the lighthouse or at one of the landing-stages. Finding no evidence of disturbance at the light or the east landing but finding some at the west – displaced railings, a dislodged stone block, and an unfastened lifebuoy – he came to the conclusion that it was there, at the west landing, that the men had met their fate.

He wrote:

> After a careful examination of the place, the railings, ropes etc., and weighing all the evidence which I could secure, I am of the opinion that the most likely explanation of the disappearance of the men is that they had all gone down on the afternoon ... to the proximity of the West landing, to secure the box with the mooring ropes etc., and that an unexpectedly large roller had come up on the Island, and a large body of water going up higher than where they were, and coming down upon them, had swept them away with resistless force.
>
> I have considered the possibility of the men being blown away by the wind, but, as the wind was westerly, I am of the opinion, notwithstanding its great force, that the more probable explanation is that they have been washed away as, had the wind caught them, it would, from its direction, have blown them up the Island and I feel certain that they would have managed to throw themselves down before they had reached the summit or brow of the Island.

There are, however, certain nagging weaknesses about this conclusion. Both the senior men's oilskins had been taken from the station, as if they had gone out with some purpose and plan. But, considering the rule that a lighthouse should not be left unmanned, all three men would not be out at the same time unless the last man were called to some dire emergency. But if such an emergency had indeed been discovered at the west landing, how could the last man, occasional keeper Donald McArthur, have been summoned to it? Neither visual signal nor cried-out sound would have reached him: the west landing was too far away and obscured from sight. Yet the facts that the kitchen chair was toppled and that McArthur's coat and wellingtons were left behind suggest that he did indeed make a dash outdoors, in his shirt-sleeves, into a freezing December day. But if he were in such a hurry, why did he then bother to shut doors and gates behind him?

It seems equally surmisable that a wave blown from the west could have thrown the men upwards and on to the incline above the cliffside, draining away to leave them high if not dry.

Which is not to say that any of the other theories is much more plausible. Some of the more superstitious Hebridean islanders contend that the keepers were whisked from their rocky outpost by sea-monsters; others blame pirates; and the most outlandish idea is that they were abducted by giant sea-birds: this doubtless inspired by the 'reincarnation' suggestion in Gibson's poem, which alludes to 'three queer black ugly birds ... like seamen sitting bolt-upright upon a half-tide reef'.

No belief has seemed too bizarre to explain the inexplicable. What about the spirit in St Flannan's Chapel, the sixth-century ruin that shares the bare plateau of Eilean Mor with the lighthouse? Surely it had been offended by the inauguration, exactly one year before, of the intrusive light-flashing monument to modern man's lack of respect for the island's sacred peace. Surely, it had simply taken its revenge!

Then there was the murder theory. Boredom and contempt-breeding familiarity had driven the men to hatred of each other. Cooped up in a small space with a wild, imprisoning sea all around them, it was only a matter of time before one of them cracked. And when it did, he went wild with violence, fighting the other two men into the sea just outside the lighthouse, then jumping in after them himself in a fit of remorse. Some credence can perhaps be accorded to this line of speculation by the fact that the bodies were never recovered. Had such an incident indeed occurred at the lighthouse area with the prevailing wind direction, the bodies would have been swept far out to sea; whereas, drowning at the lower end of the island could have seen the bodies washed up against the cliffs there.

Donald Macleod, one of the last keepers to live and work on Flannan before the light went automatic in 1971, is sure something like the struggle described above must have happened near the light station itself. 'My theory is that one of the men went berserk. One of the others tried to calm him, but found this impossible and called for help. As the third keeper ran out of the kitchen to separate his colleagues, he knocked over the chair in his haste. Then the three struggled and fell to their death.'

But another former keeper of the light –Walter Aldebert, who was there from 1953 to 1957 – preferred another story, which he painstakingly reconstructed after long hours photographically recording the frequency and height of occasional gigantic waves at the west landing. Such freak waves have always been a hazard at this point, particularly after severe storms. The west landing is in a narrow inlet ending in a cave and, when wave after wave is thundering through it, a high pressure of resident air can build up in the cave until eventually it explodes and sends tons of water washing over the cliffs. Mr Aldebert risked his life here many times to prove his conclusions which are now lodged as a report, unofficial and personal, with the Commissioners of Northern Lighthouses:

> A storm is raging and Ducat is worried about his landing ropes. Nobody goes out of a lighthouse in bad weather, but if he loses his ropes, relief may be impossible, and he must save them if he can.
>
> After the wind starts to drop ... leaving the cook ... he and the other man put on their sea boots and coats and make their way to the west side ... They come to the safety path which has a hand-rail, reaching the path which runs at right angles to the stairway and, seeing the path dry, they continue towards the crane where the box for stowing the landing ropes is situated.
>
> Suddenly a wave much bigger than the previous ones comes in and sweeps one of the men into the sea.

In a panic, the survivor races back to the light station for the third man – who knocks his chair from under him as he rushes out to help.

Grabbing a heaving line, the two men make their way back to the west side, hoping to throw the line to their unfortunate colleague. Then comes another huge wave, sweeping both men into the sea.

Despite Mr Aldebert's assiduous work on this theory, it is by no means easily accepted. Although such explosive waves can occasionally reach as high as 200 feet and even the lamphouse can be splashed with spray at over 300 feet, a wave of 100 feet – the height required to reach the men and their work platform – would be a relative rarity, and the possibility of two coming in such quick succession would be unlikely to say the least.

Yet, after all those years and all those suggestions, an absolutely convincing explanation for the men's disappearance is still teasingly elusive. For those who would still get to the bottom of the mystery, it remains regrettable that, in the absence of recovered bodies and after months of studying reports by Superintendent Muirhead and others, the Crown decided in July 1901, not to hold an inquiry. 'After careful consideration,' went the announcement, 'Crown counsel have decided to take no further proceedings.'

The case may be officially closed, but the theories keep coming thick and fast. Hugh Munro, a teacher, writer and founder of the Flannan Isles Club – which keeps relatives of the keepers and other interested parties in touch with each other – is convinced that 'there was some kind of cover-up'. He is not a romantic by nature, having once helicoptered to the island and found it 'reasonably pleasant without provoking any uncomfortably eerie feeling as Gibson's poem might have suggested'. But he instinctively feels there is something, somewhere that the public has not been informed about. And in particular, he points to an entry in the lighthouse visitors' book for 23 April 1899.

On that day, some eight months before the tragedy, one

Scott Moncrieff Penney had visited the light. His profession, 'advocate, Edinburgh', still looks conspicuously odd among the other entries by lightkeepers, seamen, works inspectors and the like. Why, wonders Munro, would he have taken the trouble to go all that way, across hazardous seas, for a social call? Wouldn't he have gone there for a professional reason?

Professor Robert Black, of Edinburgh University's department of Scots law, is more puzzled by the job description and location, as at that point in his career according to Faculty of Advocates' records, Penney was a sheriff-substitute at Portree on the Isle of Skye. Black reckons that a good reason for his visiting the light would have been as a delegate for his sheriff-principal, who might have been too busy to fulfil his visiting obligation as a commissioner of Northern Lighthouses. The professor concedes that in those days sheriffs took a more active role than they do today in the prosecution of criminal cases, but he is wary of Munro's feeling that Penney might have been visiting the light on some kind of legal business that had alarmed one of the lightkeepers. 'Did that worry,' asks Munro, 'cause that keeper to eventually crack and confess something to his mates? A confession he later regretted and decided to nullify ...?'

Munro admits that this is pure surmise, and that colleagues' pressure on such a man could not have been exactly unrelenting, as between Penney's visit and the tragedy he would have been at home for two one-month interludes after two two-month working sojourns. But no-one now seems able to say with certainty what the sheriff-substitute was doing there – the office of the Commissioners of Northern Lighthouses says it keeps no record of reasons for visits by anyone. However, the fact that Penney was accompanied on his trip by one Peter Anderson, of Lighthouse works (the only other name in the visitors' book on that date) suggests that he might have been simply checking on contractors' execution of work on the light, which had then been in operation for only four months.

Munro accepts that possibility but, instincts still nagging, suggests another theory that he finds rather seductive – the idea that the lightkeepers might have seen something they should not have seen. Perhaps a potential enemy's new, top-secret warship? Even a revolutionary British craft on offshore trials ...? 'Perhaps its officers, realising that the wrong eyes had fallen upon them, sent out a party to cleanly and efficiently remove all risk of the sighting being reported,' suggests Munro. 'This would not necessarily have meant death of course. The men could simply have been kidnapped and later incarcerated, along with their forbidden knowledge, for the rest of their lives.'

Fantastic? Maybe, though it has to be said, albeit a cliché, that stranger things have happened and that the men's disappearance in the first instance was strange enough in itself. Yet until the absolute truth is somehow miraculously discovered, even the romantics will have to settle for the mundane. For when all is said and done and all outlandish theories discounted and exhausted, Superintendent Muirhead's matter-of-fact death-by-drowning conclusion will doubtless become the accepted version of events, however unromantic its rather too logical assumption might be. And perhaps that is how it should be, for he was the man best qualified in professional and personal terms to have his opinion go down on the official record.

Indeed, he was not only a superior and colleague, but also a friend of the dead men, and had hand-picked them for their important posts on the newly-built light, designed by Robert Louis Stevenson's cousin. 'I knew Ducat and Marshall intimately,' he wrote in his report, 'and the Occasional McArthur well. I was with the keepers for a month during the summer of 1899 when everyone worked hard to secure the early lighting of the station before winter. The Board has lost two of its most efficient keepers and a competent Occasional.'

Principal keeper Ducat was forty-four years old with twenty-two years' experience in the service, and the father of four children; assistant keeper Marshall was thirty, with less than five years' experience; McArthur's age and experience were not on record, though, as a native of Lewis, he was a handy understudy – in this case for indisposed regular keeper William Ross, who was never able to return to Flannan after the tragedy.

He was not the only colleague deeply affected by it. Superintendent Muirhead himself was profoundly saddened by the affair, as the last man to see the lightkeepers alive just over a week before they vanished. His name and his wife's, appear in the visitors' book as the final guests to be entertained by the keepers. And with hindsight, it must have become a truly memorable occasion in their minds, for Muirhead concluded his report with genuinely touching words of sentiment …

I visited the Flannan Isles when the relief was made on December 7 and I have the melancholy recollection that I was the last person to shake hands with them and bid them adieu.

2   Trench's Fateful Case, 1912

Where the silvery Tay opens out to the North Sea, where the well-to-do still live in their impressive high-windowed old houses on the north-eastern outskirts of Dundee, the suburban quiet was shattered at the dying end of 1912 by the revelation of the particularly brutal and apparently motiveless murder of a rich 65-year-old spinster, Miss Jean Milne. The oh, so respectable neighbourhood was scandalized by the story. And it was to prove not only a story of one fatal tragedy, but also of a life ruined while it was still to be lived.

The killing of Miss Milne bore many similarities, disturbing but probably coincidental, to another notorious murder which had taken place in Glasgow a few years before; and not the least of these was the professional involvement of the most famous Scottish detective of his day, Detective-Lieutenant John Thomson Trench of the Glasgow City Police.

At the large Victorian mansion in Broughty Ferry where Miss Milne's body had been discovered, her head battered and her ankles bound with curtain cord, the Dundee police had found little or nothing to go on, and, swallowing their pride, felt they had no option but to yield to Trench's legendary talent and experience. The very fact that he was thus called in by the mystified local force was testament to the respect that Trench commanded among his colleagues in the Scottish police forces, though in some quarters nearer home it was to prove something of a grudging reaction, bordering dangerously on resentment …

The tenacious Western lawman arrived in what must have been to him faraway, foreign east-coast territory two days after the investigation had begun; and while he would doubtless have been flattered by the request for his services, it was a catalytic move that was to have a devastating effect on his twenty-one-year career which, up to then, had been remarkably distinguished. So admired had he been for his efficiency and consistently brilliant performance that he had even been awarded the King's Medal for meritorious service on the recommendation of his Chief Constable.

Even before he began to seek out what evidence there might be – without the benefit of Miss Milne's body, already removed for burial – Trench was drawing fateful parallels with that other case, the murder of Miss Marion Gilchrist in Glasgow in 1908, whose unsatisfactory resolution had become something of an obsession with him.

So many of the circumstances were the same: the respectable homes and the women's solitary lifestyles; the violent killings with blunt instruments (Milne with a poker, Gilchrist probably with a chair-leg); the absence of theft, despite the accessibility of money and valuables; and the fact that neither home had been forcibly entered, implying that both victims had known their killers and admitted them willingly. But it was another similarity that emerged later that was to lead to Trench's downfall ...

This was the willingness of various witnesses to come forward and swear, despite obviously less-than-perfect recall, that a mere suspect was 'definitely' the culprit. In the Gilchrist case, such witnesses had been responsible for the conviction of Oscar Slater, a Glasgow-based German gambler, and his sentencing to death for the Gilchrist murder – later commuted to life imprisonment – while other evidence that could have virtually proved his innocence was conveniently ignored. Having been deeply involved in that case, Trench was convinced that a serious miscarriage of justice had taken place; only for the sake of his job had he managed, with great difficulty, to keep his mouth shut.

But when he saw history beginning to repeat itself in the Milne case, with the overriding desire to convict bringing on a similar blindness to the facts among his peers, Trench's conscience nagged him more intensely than ever and the growing temptation to loosen his tongue on the Gilchrist case began inexorably to lead him down the road to personal disaster ...

Despite the recent appearance of modern residential developments on the early fringes of Broughty Ferry, there are still many imposing Victorian houses on, or just off, the leafy coast-hugging north road out of Dundee; and a good number of these, perched on the gentle riverbank that rolls down from the area's rich farming hinterland, command a spectacular view across the Tay to the ancient Kingdom of Fife. This is the most discreetly well-off satellite of the city, where once the beneficiaries of its nineteenth-century golden industrial age – the families of the booming jute-factory bosses, for instance – retired quietly of an evening to enjoy and contemplate the fruits of their enterprise.

Elmgrove House was one such retreat. It now has a different name and a new role, as a residential home, and its fourteen rooms are put to much more practical use than they once were – but, like so many other older residences that were built with no expense spared, the house has physically changed little since Jean Milne, sole sister and heiress of a wealthy Dundee tobacco manufacturer, lived out most of her solitary and abruptly foreshortened life within its echoing spaces. What changes there have been could only be called positive.

With its recessed gate punctuating head-high walls on a dog-leg corner of Grove Road between the high and low routes into Dundee, its boldly square architectural lines are softened by much overhanging greenery. While it is easy to imagine its looming presence behind the trees as shadowy and frightening in the days of gas street-lighting, today its once-grey stone walls have a bright surface of white paint that robs it of any lingering sinister aspect. And the gate is often wide open and, by implication, welcoming.

It was not so on Saturday, 2 November 1912, when the regular local postman found he could not get that morning's post into the overflowing letter-box. As Miss Milne had usually notified him before going on holiday in the past, his suspicions, which had been growing for some time, also overflowed – and he notified the police. One day later, after an inconclusive look at the premises the previous day – they were not over-keen to annoy the rather prickly old lady – they approached the house more determinedly. When there was no response to repeated ringing of the doorbell, a forced entry was made and, in the hall just beyond the front door, they were horrified to find the dead body of Miss Milne.

Lying at the foot of the stairs, it was fully dressed, partly covered with a sheet, and encircled by a pool of congealed blood that had obviously flowed freely from several head wounds. There was also a blood-stained poker beside it and the ankles had been tightly bound together with a cord from the nearby glass door's curtain – which had been arranged to obscure the scene from outside view. A few feet away the telephone wires had been cut, apparently with a pair of garden shears found close by.

While the dishevelled state of the hall indicated there had been a violent struggle, the binding of the ankles seemed to suggest it had not been (immediately) to the death … that the old lady's assailant had left her alive, immobilizing her only to make a getaway. But what had been the motive? Nothing appeared to have gone missing from the house and her valuable rings were not removed from her fingers, so theft was ruled out. And yet …

Miss Milne was thought to be something of an eccentric locally and certainly had some strange habits – such as the use of candles for illumination when the house was equipped with gaslighting – but the most notable thing about her was her wealth. Not only was she the owner of an extremely valuable house, inherited from her brother on his death some nine years before, but she enjoyed what was then a remarkably high income of over £1,000 a year. It was not unreasonable to assume that her death was in some way connected to her wealth … but how?

The local police were frankly baffled and, realizing the similarity of the case to that of Marion Gilchrist, quickly admitted (or at least anticipated) defeat and called in the outstanding detective whose name had come to public prominence in relation to that investigation.

Detective-Lieutenant Trench arrived in Dundee within twenty-four hours of being summoned on the Monday, but was too late to stop the burial of Miss Milne's body the next day. He wasted no time in acquiring the pathologist's report of the post-morten, however, and this showed that death had occurred soon after the injuries were inflicted; that it had been caused by a combination of shock and cerebral haemorrhage brought on by numerous blows to the head, none of which was heavy enough in itself to be fatal; and that the advanced stage of decomposition indicated that at least three weeks had passed since the attack took place.

That seemed to square reasonably well with the earliest postmark on Miss Milne's unretrieved mail – 14 October – but further enquiries began to complicate the date-of-death calculations. She was last seen alive on the 15th and on the evening of the 16th, a visiting church elder saw that the house was unusually dark and could get no response though he rang and knocked. Three nights later a trunk call from London also failed to get a reply; so it was deduced that Miss Milne must have met her demise on the night of October 15/16. However, her late brother's former gardener, Alexander Troup, later claimed that when he called at the house on 21 October to collect a contribution for charity, he saw a woman – whom he assumed to be Miss Milne – moving a curtain at an upper window. But he also failed to get a response. Neither did he succeed when he returned in the afternoon to try again. This time he noticed that the cover of the front-door lock, which in the forenoon had been down, was now up, inferring that in the mean time a key had been inserted.

This honest man's statement and other incidental details – such as the covering of the body with a sheet and the series of relatively light blows to the head – prompted a school of thought that the date of death had been later and that the culprit was a woman; but, intriguing though that theory appeared, Trench's instinct compelled him to stick with the conclusion of the autopsy, although there was something odd about that too ...

Failing to have the body exhumed, he nevertheless managed to examine the woman's clothes. He noticed several strange double punctures in them that appeared to have come from jabs by a two-pronged carving-fork – such as had been found beneath a trunk in the hall but dismissed as irrelevant – and there was no doubt that they would have made corresponding marks on the body. So why had these not been reported? Indeed, the acknowledgement of more 'light' wounds would have supported the 'female culprit' theory. Yet it remained one to which Trench could not subscribe, and gradually the evidence began to accumulate on the 'male' side.

Trench soon unearthed a significant prop to his case, which had been previously overlooked. Raking around the ashes of the dining-room grate, he recovered a partly-smoked cigar. Putting this together with the fact that just before her death the lonely Miss Milne had set the dining-room table for two, and later evidence that she had ordered a supply of wine from a local dealer 'of the same quality as my brother used to get', he consequently felt there could be no doubt about the killer's sex.

Indeed, when a reward of £100 was offered for information that would lead to the arrest of the killer, witnesses came forward thick and fast to confirm that Miss Milne had been enjoying the attentions of at least one handsome male stranger.

Two of her female friends said she had confided in them about a new man in her life and she had been so 'girlish' about it that they had concluded the relationship was a romantic one.

The maid of a neighbouring house said she had seen, from her upstairs window, a handsome six-foot-tall man in evening dress 'walking up and down' Elmgrove's garden paths one morning in the second week of October.

Elmgrove's occasional gardener recalled receiving a stranger at the house – just before Miss Milne was due to tour the Highlands in September – whom she welcomed with an excited cry: 'You have come!' He was fortyish, about 5 feet 9 inches tall, with a cheery face, fair hair and a slight fair moustache; he wore a tweed hat, was of 'gentlemanly aspect' and had a deep, guttural voice – which led the gardener to assume that he was the 'charming German' Miss Milne had mentioned meeting on one of her occasional trips to London.

Other witnesses who saw 'a strange man' around the entrance of the house included two local sisters (7 October) and a group of playing boys (11 October); but perhaps the following two were the most significant, taking account of the dates ...

A Dundee taxi-driver recalled picking up an 'English' fare from the West Station in the early hours of 15 October who wanted to go to Broughty Ferry and asked to be dropped off in the vicinity of Elmgrove. He was so agitated and 'sinister' that the cabbie was relieved to part company with him. He was about 5 feet 9 inches tall, carried a small handbag, wore an overcoat and a waterproof and had a slight fair moustache.

And a dustman claimed that, while at work in Grove Road at about 4.30 on the morning of 16 October, he had seen a bowler-hatted man come out of the house-gate ... who drew back on realizing he had been seen, then emerged again to walk briskly away and round the corner. He was tall, about thirty, with a thin pale face and a slight fair moustache.

*

Among the many confusing elements of these disparate and incomplete descriptions was the question of accents. There were German, English, and ... from the overflowing post in Miss Milne's letter-box (mostly begging-letters) the local police had retrieved something that prompted them to contact Scotland Yard about the whereabouts of 'a dashing American'. This was almost certainly a factor in the near-downfall of a certain Charles Warner, of 210 Wilton Avenue, Toronto.

When the hue and cry reached the police at Maidstone in Kent, Mr Warner happened to be in their custody; he also happened, more or less, to fit the descriptions supplied. It did not seem to matter that he had been detained for nothing more serious than the non-payment of a seven-shilling restaurant bill. Maidstone police were convinced that they had Miss Milne's murderer on their hands and promptly had him photographed. What was later to be described as 'an exceptionally bad' mugshot was then forwarded to Scotland for identification by the local witnesses.

On the strength of a general consensus of recognition among them, the chosen five – the gardener, the maid, the sisters, and the dustman – were dispatched to Maidstone to effect identification 'in the flesh'. But where was the taxi driver, with his most vital evidence? It seems he simply wasn't invited, and that was as good a reason as any for Lieutenant Trench's doubts, which had already taken root with the rough 'consensus', to start growing ...

Grateful presumably for the hospitality extended to them, which included a sightseeing tour of London, the witnesses were most co-operative at the identification parade – described by an angry Warner as 'a farce'. With the exception only of the maid, who expressed doubts about his 'too grey' hair, they all boldly pronounced the prisoner to be 'the man'. A warrant for his arrest was consequently obtained from the Dundee Sheriff and Lieutenant Trench, with the document and a pair of handcuffs in his pocket, travelled south ...

As Warner left prison after serving his fourteen days for the restaurant offence, he was surprised to be met by a huge welcoming committee which included alerted and curious public, press photographers, the local chief constable – who immediately charged him with Miss Milne's murder – and Trench, whose snapping-on of the handcuffs was accompanied by a battery of cameras clicking in unison. 'You'll be sorry for this in a few days, boys,' said Warner. 'I'm an innocent man.'

Before he and Trench left for Dundee, Warner had to suffer one more indignity – at Scotland Yard, where he was confronted with six local witnesses who claimed to have seen Miss Milne in the company of the 'dashing American' at the Strand Palace and Bonnington Hotels. In this case, not one of them was prepared to say Warner was the man. It was a different story, however, on his arrival in Scotland ...

After he appeared before the Sheriff to be formally charged – and closely examined by the curious local press, which described him as 'muscular, well-groomed and of gentlemanly appearance, with the only drawback to his attractiveness being his unshaved condition' – a fresh batch of no fewer than twenty-two 'witnesses' was produced for yet another identification exercise. Among them were the playing boys, two ladies who saw 'the man' with Miss Milne on a West Coast cruise, a local hairdresser who removed the moustache of a well-dressed man about the middle of October ... but no taxi driver. The results of this were not officially made public, but it was repeatedly stated in the press that 'a dozen witnesses' had made positive identifications.

It is not difficult to imagine what the fair-minded Lieutenant Trench must by now have been thinking, in view not only of his growing general unhappiness about the reliability of recognition sworn by so-called witnesses, but especially considering the revealing conversations he had had with Warner on their long train journey from London to Dundee's Tay Bridge station. There had been plenty of time to hear the case for the defence in the greatest of detail.

Even before he began to study the incognito 'Mr Brown' with whom he was travelling literally in tandem, Trench found himself resisting that post-arrest triumphant feeling many officers might have yielded to; for he was simply not satisfied that this was a fair cop.

Indeed, Warner protested that he had never been to Scotland in his life, and that his avoidance of the restaurant bill in Tonbridge had been prompted merely by hungry desperation after he had miscalculated his budget on a tour of France, Holland, Belgium, Antwerp, and England.

So where, asked Trench, had he been on the crucial date of 16 October?

'Antwerp,' said Warner.

'How long had you been there?' asked Trench, who by now was warming to the young Canadian who was handling his misfortune with an easy, almost jaunty air. Trench no doubt hoped this optimism was not based on a misplaced faith in himself or, worse, in British justice.

Warner replied that he had lived in the Flemish city for a week before the murder date and had left on the 17th, arriving in London on the 18th.

'Can you prove it?' asked Trench.

Warner shook his head negatively: he had been sleeping rough in parks and public places. Then he suddenly remembered that, on the relevant date, he had pawned a waistcoat in an Antwerp pawnship for one franc. Did he still have the ticket? Yes! He handed it over to Trench and knew, in a way, that he was also handing over his fate to him …

Aware that already, with statements from no fewer than a hundred witnesses, Dundee's Procurator Fiscal was submitting his prepared case to the Crown in Edinburgh for the framing of the indictment on which Warner would be brought to trial, Trench knew what he had to do – and do quickly.

Soon, he was on a train again, returning south; then travelling east by ship to Belgium's Flemish capital-of-the-north. And there, his detective's natural enterprise undeterred by the confusing network of sixteenth-century buildings, he quickly found Warner's secluded little pawnshop.

He redeemed the waistcoat, allowed himself a little self-congratulation this time, and immediately headed home again with Warner's perfect alibi tucked under his arm in a brown paper parcel. The effect, on his return, was dramatic and immediate. With the prosecution's guns so effectively spiked, the Crown Office could hardly allow the case to go ahead. It thus sent the following telegram to the Fiscal:

CHARLES WARNER ... MURDER ... CROWN COUNSEL HAVE CONSIDERED PRECOGNITIONS AND DECIDED EVIDENCE INSUFFICIENT ... PLEASE LIBERATE.

Warner's words of gratitude to Trench for the return of his waistcoat and his liberty are not on record; but this happy development was to mean a lot more to Trench than a smiling thank-you and a handshake. Though he was never to bring the true culprit to justice, the experience had proved to him that a false trail could be corrected. And perhaps that could still be achieved, however belatedly, for the wrongly convicted Oscar Slater? In that case too, there had been nothing whatsoever to connect the accused to the crime but the doubtful 'identification' of witnesses. And the Milne affair had confirmed for Trench that such evidence, while clearly worthless, could nevertheless condemn an innocent man to the gallows. Now his conscience simply would not rest ...

The postscript to this story was thus a sad one. To appreciate the irony of it, some details of the Gilchrist murder should be noted. The old lady was killed when her maid, Nellie Lambie, left the house to buy a newspaper – and returned to find a curious neighbour at the door, Arthur Adams, who had been alerted by 'chopping noises' from within. They entered the house to be confronted by a man who swept past 'like greased lightning'; and when they found the dead body of her mistress, Adams raced down into the street to give chase but could not see the man. Adams later said that Lambie did not seem surprised by the man's presence and he therefore thought that she must have known him.

This was Trench's belief too. Involved in the case from the start, he knew that Lambie had named as the intruder not Slater but another man known to her. However, something else she said had sent Trench's superiors off on a different trail from which they were not to be deflected by mere logic. The only valuable item missing from the house, she claimed, was a diamond crescent brooch. And it was discovered that Slater had been trying to sell a pawn ticket for such a brooch around the gaming-houses he frequented.

This was surely their man! Not only did he live near the murder scene, but he had been known to use several different names and had also suddenly left Glasgow for New York. The inconvenient facts that the brooch 1) when recovered from the pawnship, did not resemble the stolen one, and 2) had been pawned long before the murder, were simply brushed aside. Slater was brought back from America and charged with Marion Gilchrist's murder. Now Nellie Lambie, and several other witnesses, were prepared to say he was the man, though Arthur Adams was more cautious.

No-one was interested in Trench's protests, or Slater's for that matter – 'My lord, I know nothing about the affair, you are convicting an innocent man' – and the prisoner was sentenced to be hanged on 27 May 1909. Though massive public protests were perhaps responsible for this being commuted to life imprisonment two days before it was carried out, the bewildered man was taken to Peterhead Prison where, as Convict No. 1992, he was to spend nearly two decades begging for justice.

Although several distinguished pens fought bravely to expose the flaws in the prosecution's case against him – including those of the famous criminologist William Roughead and the 'Sherlock Holmes' author Sir Arthur Conan Doyle – nothing was done in high places for Oscar Slater as the early years of his imprisonment passed. He was not to know that his best champion was to be a Glasgow policeman who, after the Broughty Ferry affair, was about to put his distinguished career on the line for him …

Indeed, initially, Trench himself did not even know that. He knew, of course, that to challenge his police superiors directly would be perceived as an unforgivable professional sin – as would an approach over their heads to a higher authority. But it was a straight choice. And reckoning that the first course would find stony ground in any case, what he had to do was pursue the latter with 'safety' guarantees attached. Eventually, a prominent lawyer, David Cook, persuaded a prison commissioner to put Trench's plea discreetly to Scottish Secretary McKinnon Wood. The response – 'If the constable mentioned will send me a written statement of the evidence in his possession, I will give this matter my best consideration' – led the detective to believe that he could impart his information with impunity.

He was utterly and naïvely wrong.

Though Cook pressured the Scottish Secretary into setting up an enquiry into the Slater case, this was commonly seen as a farce. When its results were later published as a parliamentary paper, it was riddled with asterisks where evidence had been deemed inconvenient and the key name of the man first given by Lambie appeared only as initials. A name still much argued about in Glasgow.

Trench recalled how a niece of Miss Gilchrist quoted

Lambie thus, just after the murder: 'Oh, Miss Birrell, I think it was AB. I know it was AB.'

And he mentioned a visit to Lambie when he 'touched on AB', asking if she really thought this was the man she saw. 'Her answer was: "It's gey funny if it wasn't him I saw".' Yet both these witnesses now denied ever having made such statements and, to compound Trench's predicament, one Glasgow policeman after another came forward to discredit his evidence.

As the farce ended, on 25 April, Trench's troubles really began. With no action being taken on Slater's conviction, the detective was suspended from duty three months later, the case going before the Glasgow magistrates along with this statement from his Chief Constable: 'It is contrary to public policy and to all police practice for an officer to communicate to persons outside the police force information which he has acquired in the course of his duty, without the express sanction of the chief officer of his force.'

Trench defended himself and his altruistic motives rubustly, but even production of the Scottish Secretary's letter asking for his information failed to save him. He was dismissed with ignominy from the Glasgow police on 14 September 1914. And even an appeal to McKinnon Wood had no effect – the Scottish Secretary did not even bother to respond to his letter.

So surely his enemies in the force were satisfied now? Not so, it appeared. Although he enlisted in the Royal Scots Fusiliers to start building a new career for himself, his ex-colleagues were not yet finished with John Thomson Trench. As a parting shot, they mounted what was later described as a 'vindictive' prosecution against him and the lawyer Cook, accusing them of receiving stolen goods while Trench was with the force. But this time they were thwarted. The judge dismissed the case, saying that the men, who had been concerned with returning the goods to their rightful owners, had actually acted with 'meritorious intention'.

Yet the once-great detective never recovered from the double-shock. Though he served his regiment well throughout the Great War with the rank of quartermaster-sergeant, he died at the age of fifty, on the fourth anniversary of his arrest. He did not, therefore, live to see Oscar Slater released some ten years later ...

On 10 November 1927, the then-Scottish Secretary Sir John Gilmour finally gave in to a new and relentless pressure from the media to authorize Slater's release, already overdue in terms of the average span of 'life'. But if Sir John were expecting applause for the decision, he did not get it. Even as a relieved, if disbelieving, Slater was telling the press 'I want rest, I want rest' – outside the Glasgow rabbi's home to which he had been invited to pick up his life again – the pressure was renewed, this time for an appeal hearing to clear Slater's name. Again, the authorities yielded, and at last the original court judgement was 'set aside'.

Disappointingly for Slater, who hoped to be unequivocally cleared, this was based on a technicality; yet he received £6,000 compensation. He owed a lot to Sir Arthur Conan Doyle, who had campaigned for him to the end, but they fell out, and his gratitude, in the form of a £200 gift, was focused on an equally deserving sympathizer, journalist William Park. An old friend of Trench, he was the man largely responsible for the last catalytic barrage of pressure with the publication of his book, *The Truth About Oscar Slater*.

He was also the only man who fully realized the contribution of his friend, acknowledged in the book's dedication with words that ring as a fitting epitaph to a man who gave his life to justice but received little of it in return:

Dedicated to the memory of the late Lieutenant John T. Trench, King's Medallist, Glasgow, who, as a public officer of the police force, actuated by an inspiring sense of justice, sacrificed his career and pension in a personal attempt to rescue from a life's detention in prison, and with a desire to save others from the risk of a similar cruel fate, a man whom he believed on his conscience to have been wrongly convicted in the Scottish High Court of Justiciary, and for which noble act he was dismissed and ruined.

3   Gone in the Night, 1929

Now in his seventies, crofter Calum Cameron turns his weather-beaten face away from the questioner, looks to the heavens in exasperation, and closes his eyes to the bright sunshine. It is understandable. He is obviously a man who enjoys and craves for peace. And his life – lived out in a simple two-storey cottage with four dormer windows looking out over a sandy inlet to the open sea – would have been delightfully, remotely quiet, even by the standards of the holy island of Iona, were it not for that fateful night in November 1929, when his parents' boarder, Norah Emily Farnario, walked out into the darkness clutching a knife in her hand.

He was only twelve years old at the time, growing up in what many would consider an idyllic setting: a playground of gardens and fields, rocks and beaches, animals and fishing; in a world of his own set apart (by perhaps half a mile) from what is still today a small and close-knit community of village cottages along the shorefront where the little ferry comes in across the one-and-a-half-mile Sound of Iona from Fionnphort on Mull. No doubt he also ventured further, along the encircling island track, to the large green mound of Fairy Hill, said to harbour the spirits of the pre-Christian dead; the mystic mound that seemed to fascinate Miss Farnario so.

At first sight, viewed from the ferry, the island of Iona seems nothing much more than pleasingly pretty. In contrast to the elemental and mountainous magnificence of its near-neighbour Mull, it is small, green and low and, were it not for its silver sands, handsomely restored abbey and historic founding role in the establishment of Christianity in Scotland – St Columba and twelve companions landed there in 563 – it would be but a pleasant, unimportant dot on the map of Scotland.

With its many landmarks bearing deep and sometimes puzzling significance in the history of religion, the island has become a place of pilgrimage not only for believers and students of theology from all over the world, but also for simply interested tourists. Rather than openly welcomed, their continuing and growing influx is philosophically tolerated by the resident islanders – fewer than a hundred – who are by nature reticent and matter-of-fact and practise their own faith in that modest spirit.

While the presence of the young Iona Community may compound this slightly uneasy mix, its spiritual idealism is remarkably effective in breathing new life into the island. The abbey, lovingly restored, is a haven for people once more; and the little school that almost died a few years ago is filling up again and echoing to the cries of human regeneration behind the ruins of the ancient nearby nunnery. But Iona was not so lively and cosmopolitan when Miss Farnario, accompanied by a lady friend who would soon leave her to her own fateful devices, made her pilgrimage from London in August 1928 – then it was still an island in the truest sense of the word, far from anywhere, without basic amenities and communication systems.

Paradoxically, that probably uplifted the tall, rather intense young woman in hand-woven clothes as, after more than two days of travelling, she and her companion stepped off the ferry into a different world, yet one which she at least imagined she knew well, for her basic motivation for making the daunting journey to Iona was the belief that she had been on the island in a prevous incarnation. She intended to stay for an indefinite period to seek the peace and serenity that had eluded her in London and, as she made her way along the shorefront to the house of Mrs Macdonald where she would be boarding, no doubt she felt some of that already washing over her. She would use the quiet to write about, and pursue her study of, telepathy, faith-healing and other mystic subjects. She would use it also to find some quietness in herself. But that was not to be.

Norah Farnario, the 32-year-old troubled daughter of an Italian doctor and an English gentlewoman, may have physically escaped from the city, but she was not to struggle free from the dark forces that inhabited her own mind. These came with her like so much unwanted baggage; and if she had hoped to find a place whose force for peace would do battle with and overcome the demons, she had come to the wrong place.

Superficially perhaps, Iona exudes serenity but it is a strangely powerful peace. As Kenneth Clark wrote in *Civilisation*, when trying to capture the potency of the island's atmosphere, 'I never come to Iona without the feeling that "some god is in this place".'

And Mrs Alison Johnson, of the St Columba Hotel on the track up to the abbey, puts it this way: 'Iona is a strong place. It can attract some "interesting" types and, if people are a little unbalanced when they arrive here, it can overbalance them completely.'

Certainly, something like that happened to the darkly attractive Miss Farnario – for, far from finding inner quiet in the simple life in Iona, she seemed to suffer increasing mental anguish the longer she stayed. She was always restless. After her companion departed, she moved from her lodgings in the east to Traighmor, the Camerons' relatively isolated croft perhaps half-a-mile to the south-west of the main cluster of village houses. But despite its delightful location, set back from a small, craggy bay behind a hundred-yard expanse of lush grass, she could find no peace there either.

By day, she was often to be seen sitting down by the

shore writing; and although her thoughts were obviously deep and obsessional, she never attempted to impose them upon either islanders or visitors, to whom she was friendly, charming and consequently well liked. When she felt she could, she would mix freely among them, and she appreciated the fact that they respected her privacy. Yet, however comfortable and popular she became with them, she remained less than comfortable with herself.

For by night, it was a different and less congenial story. She went out, with increasing frequency, on lonely walks to study the island's ancient, mysterious mounds and stones, apparently fuelling her already volatile preoccupation with spiritualism and the occult. Given the atmospheric power of the place even by day, perhaps it was not surprising that the forces of darkness came down heavily upon her. She seemed, almost, to be asking for trouble and was particularly fascinated by the mound known in the Gaelic as Sithean Mor, the Fairy Hill, a grassy knoll just south of the extremity of the road leading to The Machair, a tract of arable land in the middle west of the island. As its ancient name suggests, the mound is one of several knolls of pre-Christian times in Iona where, according to legend, the fairies or angels would revel while passing mortals heard the faint strains of their music emanating from within. Here also, a prying monk is said to have witnessed St Columba himself in communion with the angels – 'Clad in white garments, they came flying to him with wonderful speed,' relates his biographer Adomnan, 'and stood round the holy man as he prayed.' Here also, Norah Farnario joined the angels.

Interviewed after that sad event, her housekeeper in the family home at Mortlake Road, Kew – a Miss Varney – described her mistress as 'a woman of extraordinary character who claimed to cure people by telepathy' and who, despite being quite cheerful and happy much of the time, would 'moan and cry out piteously' if she were not allowed to heal someone she had perceived as having a curable problem. Once, she had announced her intention of fasting for forty days but was persuaded to give up after two weeks. Occasionally, she 'went off into trances for several hours'.

Indeed, Miss Farnario is said to have told her hosts at Traighmor that they should not be alarmed if she should go into a trance for as long as a week. Not surprisingly, Calum's family began to wonder about their endearing but ever-more-disturbed young guest from London. Apart from her strange nocturnal walks, there was her increasingly agitated demeanour that manifested itself in growing dishevelment; incoherent references to visions and spiritual messages; the fact that her curtains were never drawn because she believed she could see the faces of her previous 'patients' in the clouds; and the two oil lamps that she kept burning in her room throughout the night. She did not, apparently, get much sleep. If she were not out walking, she would write voluminously by the light of these lamps far into the night and was often so exhausted by dawn that she would then go to bed for the rest of the day. When she seemed particularly overwrought, the Camerons would consider calling a doctor – but were specifically warned against that by their guest. Presumably because of her convictions, or perhaps because of some difference with her doctor-father, she had no time for the standard practitioners of orthodox medicine.

It was thus difficult to know what precisely was ailing her. Many islanders were acquainted with her but few, if any, got near her innermost thoughts; and in the absence of some qualified medical enlightenment, the villagers could do no more than hazard guesses at her condition. Despite their undeniable sympathy for her, some of these were, and still are, less than respectful. At the very least, she was considered to have a severe persecution complex. But did she even know herself what the problem was? To her, no doubt, the demons inside her head were more than imaginings. She behaved as if she were being hunted, and if her pursuers were not evil spirits of her own creation, who … or what … were they?

In any case, the hunting was to come to an abrupt and shocking conclusion as the winter of 1929 drew in.

It must have been something of a relief to the Camerons when, on Sunday, 17 November, their guest rose unusually early and dramatically announced that she would have to leave the island, having received messages to that effect 'from the world beyond'. But when the Camerons realized that she intended to go immediately, they warned her that this would be impossible: there were no ferries running on the Sabbath. This did not seem to get through to her until, packed up and standing by the shore, she saw for herself – gazing across the Sound to Mull – that there was no way she could get off the island that day. Frightened and dejected, she returned to the cottage, announced that she had had another call and was not now leaving, then locked herself in her room. When she reappeared briefly before going to bed, however, the hunted look was gone and she seemed unusually rational and normal. 'Aye,' recalls Calum, 'she was a' right on the Sunday night.'

But she was certainly not all right the next morning. When Calum's sister took breakfast to her room, she did not answer the knock. There was a smell of burning, so the girl entered, to find the room empty. The bedclothes were turned down from the pillows, the oil lamps near her typewriter were still alight, and the fireplace was filled with burned papers and pamphlets. All her clothing was still in the room and such personal belongings as her watch, rings, and hairpins lay neatly on the dressing-table. Nothing appeared to be missing ...

The Camerons, alarmed, immediately searched the neighbourhood and whistled for her along the shore where she had been in the habit of sitting writing. But there was no trace of their lonely lodger. Remembering that she had 'gone missing' before, they then waited for a few hours – perhaps she'd just over-extended one of her nocturnal walks – before summoning a group of neighbourly helpers, whose efforts also proved fruitless.

She was still missing when darkness fell, and next morning the search, now scaled up with official police organization from Mull and more island volunteers, got under way again.

But it was not until the Tuesday afternoon that the breakthrough came. Alerted by their excited collie, two farmers announced that they had seen 'something white' on the side of Fairy Hill. And when the searchers drew close, they gasped with shock at the sight of Norah Farnario's naked body. A *Glasgow Bulletin* 'informant' described the scene like this:

> The body was lying in a sleeping posture on the right side, the head resting on the right hand. Round the neck was a silver chain and cross. A few feet away a knife was found.
>
> Miss Farnario had left the Camerons' farmhouse (about a mile away) sometime during Sunday night. The island was bathed in moonlight and a very keen frost prevailed. The doctor who was called gave it as his opinion that death was due to exposure.
>
> With the exception of a few scratches on the feet, caused by walking over the rough ground, there were no marks on the body.

And a reporter for the *Oban Times* gave this version:

> Her body, which was unclothed, was discovered lying on a large cross which had been cut out of the turf, apparently with a knife which was lying by, and round her neck was a silver chain and cross. Death was apparently due to exposure.

Other accounts further elaborated the basic facts. Such as: She was not completely naked – she wore a black cloak decorated with occult insignia. The silver chain around her neck was no longer silver – it had turned black. She had taken the 'long' steel knife in the age-old belief that the simple act of carrying a blade would ward off evil spirits – it was not lying beside her but had to be forcibly removed from her tightly clutched fingers. Alternatively, some suggest the knife was for fending off a real rather than an imagined danger. After all, 'the balls of her feet were badly bruised' as if she had been desperately running away from something or someone. It was rumoured that a 'man in a cloak' had been seen in the vicinity ...

There were many more highly developed theories, but Calum Cameron, in his down-to-earth way, has always shrugged off fanciful speculation. 'It was just an ordinary kitchen knife,' he says, 'which could have done no harm to anybody.' He is clearly not impressed by the knife-for-defence theory and believes her fate was sealed only by the frost. 'She just died of exposure as the doctor said, it's that simple.' So the knife was only for cutting that symbolic cross in the turf? 'There was no cross,' he claims. 'She was just digging in the ground, maybe trying to get to the fairies inside. She was a disturbed woman, that's all.'

Indeed, foul play was ruled out and the cause of death was officially stated to be 'heart failure'. But others have found the story of Miss Farnario's bizarre death less easy to explain, one of these being her London housekeeper, who was clearly perplexed by the prescient note she received from her mistress two days before her death. It said simply:

> My dear Miss Varney – Do not be surprised if you do not hear from me for a very long time. I have a terrible healing case on.

One writer has examined the theory that Miss Farnario was the victim of 'psychic murder'. Having dabbled in spiritualism, theosophy, thought-reading and faith-healing to the point of joining the Alpha and Omega occult group, she also became friendly with the wife of Samuel Lidell Mathers, a leading light of another group of occultists called The Golden Dawn. The alleged penalty for breaking this group's oath of silence was to be subjected to 'a current of will' which would cause the offender 'to fall dead or paralysed as if blasted by lightning'.

So had the victim been so indiscreet as to make herself the target of what a leading figure in the occult world called an 'astral attack'? Was her increasingly agitated behaviour caused by some perceived threat of such a fate? Was she pursued by the cloaked man to her death? Did she commit a kind of passive suicide? The answers are now buried with Norah Emily Farnario in the graveyard of kings at St Odhrain's chapel in the grounds of Iona Abbey, where a tiny, mossy open-book memorial yields only the words:

N.E.F. Aged 33. 19th Nov 1929

She was interred three days after being found. Through papers discovered in her room, an uncle and aunt were contacted in London but no member of her family was able to undertake the journey to Scotland, and a solicitor was sent to make the necessary arrangements. In contrast, the tragedy and pathos of the young woman's death had so aroused the sympathies of the islanders that – according to a visitor's account – 'practically every soul on Iona attended her impressive funeral'.

While the mysteries of her harrowing life and death may have gone with her, what is certain is that the troubled young lady who went to seek peace in Iona did finally find it there; the ultimate peace.

4   Death of a Warship, 1940

He was but a short-trousered lad then, head down in his classroom at St Mary's School, earnestly getting down to serious work after a playful lunch-break. But when the huge explosion occurred, like a great thunder cracking across the River Clyde less than a mile-and-a-half away, he was immediately on his feet again, shocked and confused and ready to run. He couldn't understand what was happening as the windows of the schoolroom blew a shattering of glass inwards across the desks and his classmates screamed.

'We didn't realize the implications of it at the time,' recalls Tony McGlone; and neither did his teacher, whose name he can't recall, though her unflappability made its mark on his memory. 'She ordered us all to stay put, stay calm, and we tried to keep on working, but it was difficult; and as soon as school was out, we all ran down to the esplanade to see what had caused the huge bang.'

What Tony McGlone and his schoolmates beheld that Tuesday afternoon, gazing in transfixed shock across the water from the riverbank road that skirts the gritty old shipbuilding town of Greenock – of which he was to become the provost in later life – was a pall of smoke risking from a large warship in the naval anchorage off Princes Pier. They were by no means the only onlookers: many local shops had taken a half-day holiday and it seemed as if the whole population of the town had gathered to watch. They saw the estuary alive with 'chaotic' drama-charged activity. Other big ships, having weighed anchor and moved away to safer waters, had sent small launches to assist in the rescue operations. But already the situation looked bad. The stricken ship was, recalls Tony McGlone, 'well on fire and listing badly' as rescue teams tried desperately to snatch her crewmen to safety before she broke up and sank. It was to be a losing battle, with a tragic toll of many young lives, and Tony still remembers how, long after the war, 'you could still see her remaining mast and the top of one of her funnels protruding from the water'.

The date was 30 April 1940, and what he had witnessed was the frantic aftermath of the mysterious (self?)-destruction of the *Maille Brézé*, a 2,440-ton French Cassard class destroyer, which had come to 'rest' in the Clyde after acquitting herself with honour at the Battle of Narvik. In this critical episode of the war, both British and French had been attempting to prevent the fall of Norway by landing British troops on its coast. The *Maille Brézé* had fought alongside British vessels, helping to knock out all eight German destroyers engaged against them, to effect what turned out to be a too-brief Allied landing. She was one of four French destroyers to be mentioned in dispatches for the brave and skilful performance of her 220-strong crew.

It was thus supremely ironic that, having survived such a bruising and decisive battle, she was to meet a surprisingly violent end in the friendly and relatively peaceful waters of the Clyde, a few miles west of Glasgow. She had arrived three days before, along with a couple of Royal Navy warships, to enjoy the naval equivalent of a boxer's pause between rounds: the most welcome part of conflict ... the clean-up and refreshment ... which in maritime terms meant refuelling, replenishing, re-ammunitioning, and general maintenance. There should have been nothing dangerous in that. So how did the ship suddenly explode and, consequently, lose a large number of her young crewmen in an agonizing death?

Among her impressive array of armaments, the

eight-year-old *Maille Brézé* boasted six 21.7-inch torpedo
tubes, and it was generally reported by survivors that
during maintenance work on one of these, 'something
happened' ... a torpedo came adrift, flew out of the tube,
skidded along the deck, and collided with the lower
structure of the bridge – causing the enormous explosion
that reverberated throughout Greenock and for as much
as ten miles beyond.

For the many brave local people who, on hearing it,
dashed to the scene without hesitation – all kinds of small
vessels hurriedly cast off from Princes Pier and Albert
Harbour to join forces with the professionals' boats from
the nearby warships – there was no time to ask: why?
Dunkirk was yet two months away, but its spirit was
already to be seen here as waves of wounded crewmen,
many of them badly burned, were ferried to safety. Some
were taken to other ships at anchor; others were treated
immediately on the small boats even as they were being
taken ashore; and by the time the first casualties reached
land, ambulances were waiting to take them to hospital.

Even when there was a gap in the ambulance relays,
succour was at hand. A general alert having been sent out
to Air Raid Protection posts, dozens of volunteers,
including many nurses, were standing by at the docks to
administer first aid to the injured. The close-knit
community of Greenock was pulling out all the stops. For
the shocked but not too badly hurt, a comfort station was
set up in the Greenock Temperance Institute, where local
women, with perspiration pouring down their faces,
ministered to the young Frenchmen as if they were their
own sons. Hot drinks and plates of food were handed out
continually, and even an interpreter was produced – Mrs
McGill, a Frenchwoman who had married a Greenock
man. But, as a local newspaper put it when recording the
event five years later after the lifting of wartime
censorship: 'Frenchman and Scot did not need to speak a
common language that day. Each knew what the other
wanted, and many a Frenchman, by a silent handshake,

"spoke" more deeply of his gratitude than in words.' In response to the dreadful event, the best side of human nature had emerged in a tragic kind of triumph. Brotherly love, compassion and courage were rising up everywhere ...

For some, however, there was to be no salvation; no joyful landing on shore; no chance to express their gratitude for local people's courage. For as the catalogue of dramas unfolded, it became clear that a number of unfortunate sailors on the *Maille Brézé* had somehow got themselves hopelessly trapped below – in the for'ard mess-deck near the potentially lethal unflooded main magazine – and their chances of being saved were minimal. Indeed, their grim plight so perplexed their would-be rescuers that old men are, to this day, moved to tears by the memory. It had been truly unbearable to witness, for it transpired that there was simply no way to save the men, no way they could be brought out of the holocaust ... because the forecastle hatch from the deck had been buckled by the first explosion and fire raged between them and the bulkhead door leading aft. The final horror of the situation was that, while a few of them could stick their heads out of the portholes to gasp hysterically for air, the holes were simply too small for the slimmest of men to crawl through.

As it was, frustrated by their own powerlessness in the face of the French sailors' harrowing screams for help, the rescuers soon began clutching at straws. A desperate plan emerged to cut through the ship's hull with oxy-acetylene gear; but as a group of suitably-equipped men approached on the duty cutter from HMS *Warspite*, they were waved away by a British officer who had boarded the blazing ship. Lieutenant D.S. Johnston, from HMS *Furious*, reckoned there was too little time to effect such a precarious and complicated operation successfully, and the danger of a blow-back that would cost more lives was too great. Things obviously looked even worse from the vantage point he had courageously climbed to, the better to assess the situation ...

And he wasn't alone. With shells from the ready-use lockers looping and bursting all around them, he and four other Royal Navy men – including Lieutenant R.H. Roberts, a probationary temporary-surgeon – had risked their own lives to shin up the ship's massive anchor chain from their own small boat and lever themselves over the high, red-hot bow. They reckoned that from there, with a brisk northerly breeze sweeping the fire aft along the hull that was lying north-and-south in the estuary, they would at least be able to see how and who they could help.

But it did not look good from the moment they stepped on deck. One of the boarding sailors, Able Seaman Robert McCaw, made straight for the jammed forecastle hatch cover and optimistically applied his brute strength to it; but it simply refused to budge and, as his fingers began to burn unbearably, he had to admit defeat. He stood up with a deep sigh and addressed his eyes to Johnston: what now? Confronted with danger and distress from all angles – the suffocating French sailors beseeching them for help from the portholes; the unexploded main magazine threatening them from below; a torpedo warhead burning but not exploding a few feet away – the lieutenant realized that very little could be done. And the decision was up to him. He looked at Roberts the surgeon, already preparing his hypodermic needle and morphine phials, and with an air of grim resignation reluctantly gave him the go-ahead.

The doctor took off his uniform jacket, stretched his body out and over the searing edge of the deck, and called out to the men below: would they please extend their arms – not their heads – from the portholes? When his intention was understood, there was a general scuffling and crying, 'like trapped rats tearing at each other to get away first,' it was said later. But who could blame them? A more dreadful fate by far was fast overtaking them. Roberts grabbed the first arm, squeezed home the sedative, and pulled himself back quickly to roll over and reload the syringe. Then he took another, pulled back and reloaded; then another ... until, after a few dying cries, all at once the ship fell ominously silent. Together, the hypnotic sedative and the overpowering heat and fumes from the holocaust had finally done their work. 'At about 1600 hours,' it was later reported to the Admiralty, 'there were no living men inboard.'

It might not have brought about a joyful resolution, but surgeon Roberts' remarkable act of mercy was to be long remembered as one of the most heroic episodes of that fateful day; at the very least it had brought blessed, ultimate relief to many desperate men facing a horrific end. Little wonder that, equally, it had been a relief to him and his fellow-rescue workers to hear no more the agonized moans and screams of the hapless victims as they finally succumbed to the roasting heat and deadly fumes. Doubtless, they would have preferred a quick end; but such was the contrary mood of the gods that disastrous day, the one miracle that took place only made things worse for the trapped men: they must have wondered why, amid all the fires of hell, the nearby unflooded main magazine – only recently restocked with a potent mix of shells, torpedo warheads and depth-charges – had not blown up and blasted them away with one merciful blow.

But there was a deal more courage to be seen that day; not least among the men of the regular fire brigade and civilian Auxiliary Fire Service. For meanwhile, although she showed little outward sign of it, the *Maille Brézé* was burning furiously and her plight had become more serious with repeated secondary explosions caused by igniting magazines. Archie Sweeney, a relatively new recruit to the AFS, was among the scores of firemen ferried out on fifteen drifters, over more than a mile of choppy water, to douse the stricken ship's super-heated structure. 'There was a high wind blowing and it was rather difficult to come alongside her – you could feel the heat from the hull even out in the open air. However, once we'd managed to tie up so many drifters on either side, we got the pumps into operation and very shortly we were pumping thousands of gallons of water a minute into the ship.' Though they were keenly aware of the dangers – not least of more ammunition going up at any time – the firemen selflessly ignored them as they battled on, some of them boarding the vessel and finding the heat from the plates was burning their boot-leather through to the flesh.

In fact the whole exercise was a very high-risk gamble: their actions would either kill the fire (and thus save the ship) or, if the blaze refused to die, they would cause her to sink. For although much of their hosed-on water turned instantly to steam, the more they poured into her, the heavier she got and the greater became the likelihood of her sinking. And as time went on, it seemed the latter result had become a distinct probability. Yet the firemen stuck doggedly to their posts until it was depressingly obvious that they could do no more.

The moment was signalled by the order to abandon ship, issued shortly before eight in the evening. The ship's back was broken, one of her funnels had toppled over, the mizzen mast was sheared; and when her decks became awash, it was clear she could no longer be saved. But just as the disconsolate men clambered off the ship and on to their homebound vessels, their valour was challenged again. Archie Sweeney takes up the story:

> As we were drawing away from the ship, two French petty officers appeared on the scene wearing fire helmets ... and asking for five men to give them some assistance. The person next to me suggested that we shouldn't be yellow, and he immediately jumped back on the ship; I did likewise, and so did another fireman. So the situation then was that we were standing on the deck of a ship that was going down rather rapidly, and all the drifters had left us – so we were isolated.

Trying not to think about their perilous position, the three volunteers asked what they could do to help and the officers suggested that they try to release the anchor chain – 'presumably to enable the sinking bow to come up, though I wasn't sure that was a good idea' – but even as they made their way towards it, they realized there was no hope: that they were now in very deep trouble, with no means of saving themselves. 'Things were beginning to look rather dangerous,' recalls Archie with considerable understatement. 'The water was rising very rapidly now, and the deck was at quite a severe angle.' Was the three men's bravery about to cost them their lives? Had they volunteered only for a watery grave? It certainly looked like it, but amazingly, at the last moment, their prayers were answered. They could hardly believe their eyes as ...

'Suddenly, from nowhere, a little motor boat with two French sailors on board drew alongside, and they waved to us to jump on board.' Up to their knees in water washing over the big ship's deck, Archie and his mates waded gratefully over to the edge of the deck; but at that critical point one of them suddenly froze on the spot, a non-swimmer unable to make the leap across the swirling vortex of water between the two vessels. 'I was actually the last to leave,' says Archie, 'because in the end I just had to push him off.'

Thanking their incredible luck, they breathed again as the motor boat turned sharply and sped off in a swirl of white water. Behind them, they watched the great ship's head gradually slip under the lapping waves to come to rest on a sandbank, fortuitously clear of both the commercial and naval shipping channels. And as they stepped ashore at Gourock pier in the darkness – it was now about eleven at night – their relief was tempered with a feeling of deep sadness: not because, like all local men, they cared inordinately for ships; but because they knew that still on board the sunken vessel, entombed by layers of twisted metal and freezing depths of water, were the bodies of many men who had not been so lucky as they. And just how many they could not be sure.

In fact, the overall toll at the end of the day the *Maille Brézé* sank turned out to be much worse than anyone had expected: Forty-seven hospitalized, six killed outright by the explosion on the upper deck, and no fewer than twenty-eight burned, suffocated or drowned below decks. Their bodies were not recovered until the *Maille Brézé* was finally salvaged in 1954, and the sight of them in their last contortions so shocked one of the divers involved that he could no longer take on that kind of work. The bodies of the six sailors who died instantly – because they were close to, or working on, the ill-fated torpedo tube – were buried in the shadow of an old evergreen tree in Greenock cemetery soon after the ship's demise; later to be joined by those of three others who did not recover in hospital. And until they were exhumed and returned to France in 1948, their presence served constantly to remind local people not only of the tragic end of the *Maille Brézé* but also of the bewildering mystery of it all. They knew, roughly, how it had happened – but why?

Who or what could have caused the release of the exploding torpedo on that awful day of death and destruction? Had battle fatigue among the crewmen caused routine safety precautions to be forgotten or ignored? And even if that were the case, what about the automatic fail-safe mechanism that should have prevented any torpedo from firing when facing inboard? For the device to have failed in conjunction with momentary carelessness by the relevant maintenance artificer seems a circumstance almost too coincidental to be credible. 'Sabotage' was one of the first words to sweep along the Greenock waterfront almost as soon as the explosion was heard; and despite the wisdom of reflective hindsight and official post-mortems upholding the generally-accepted conclusion that the incident was simply an unfortunate accident, there will always be a nagging suspicion that there was indeed a sinister hand behind the disaster. And because those who were nearest to the incident did not survive to tell their version of the tale, there will always be a variety of theories as to whose hand that might have been.

In the year that the Free French were to succumb to the invading German armies, there was much suspicion of the pro-German French – soon to become known as Vichyites – and one of the first local conclusions was that a secret sympathizer on board the *Maille Brézé* might have quietly arranged for the torpedo to malfunction.

Then there were the Nazis themselves. Having failed to knock out the hard-fighting destroyer with their heavy naval hardware at the Battle of Narvik, they might well have reckoned it an easier exercise by far to deliver an audacious fatal blow to her by means of one man's clandestine stealth.

Such imaginative thoughts were refuted dismissively by local naval security officers at the time, who nevertheless managed to add their own dimension of mystery to the matter by pointing out that 'this is a top-secret business'. But whatever the truth was, her destruction was so traumatic and complete that no enemy agent could have done it better. The *Maille Brézé* died no less spectacular death than she would have met in the raging heat of battle; and if the responsibility did indeed rest with one of her own crew, no doubt the enemy indulged in a grim smile of satisfaction at the strange fate of the destroyer which, ostensibly and ironically, succeeded in destroying herself.

5   A Royal Disaster, 1942

On the rugged, undulating heights near Eagle's Rock, neither David Morrison nor his son Hugh could see the source of it, but the alarmingly close engine noise in the sky above them made the shepherds stop work on rounding-up their sheep and stare up into the densely unrevealing mist. The roar passed overhead, faded slightly, then exploded into a thundercrack that told them, without doubt, that a large aircraft had come to grief not far away. And there was still more noise. As father and son looked askance at each other, oblivious to their sheep scattering in fright, the grinding, breaking sound seemed to go on and on until it turned into another enormous explosion – which they were to learn later was the noise of two-and-a-half thousand gallons of aviation fuel blowing up.

It was the early afternoon of Tuesday, 25 August 1942, and what they, and a lone angler not far away, had just heard was soon to reverberate all around the United Kingdom and the world. But the basic, shocking fact that made this accident on a remote Caithness hillside different from the hundreds of similar wartime tragedies – if it were indeed an accident – was not to become known until the wreckage of the plane, a Royal Air Force Sunderland flying-boat W-4026, was found after many hours of mist-hampered searching by parties from the nearby communities of Dunbeath, Berriedale, and Wick. They had been alerted by both the angler and young Hugh Morrison who, after his initial shock, had reacted quickly by sprinting down the hill, jumping onto his motor bike, and racing off to raise the alarm.

In some places during their difficult search visibility in the mist was down to about fifteen feet, and some of the rapidly-recruited farmers, gillies and special constables found themselves depending entirely on their sense of smell to lead them to their target. First to find the smouldering wreckage of the plane was farmer James Sutherland. It was a shocking sight – shattered into thousands of pieces, with the bodies of several of its occupants strewn around it. One of them, though still clad in a flying suit, wore a uniform with the ring of an air commodore on the sleeve. His face looked familiar to Sutherland and the friend he had immediately summoned to the location just north of Braemore Falls, shepherd James Gunn (whose son, a schoolboy at the time, still remembers how 'we even caught the smell of the crash at the school, although we didn't know where it was coming from'). Sutherland, Gunn and several other searchers who had now gathered at the spot soon became heroes as, despite their fears about the danger of the still-burning wreck with its potentially explosive cargo, they decided to approach and search it, one man declaring, 'To hell with bombs, there may be people still alive in there.'

But their own vote for hero of the hour went to the seventy-year-old Dr Kennedy from Dunbeath who, after driving about eight miles and traversing another four miles of desolate moorland on foot, turned out to be what a local writer later called 'an industrious and inspiring leader'. Being more accustomed to dealing with death than the others – who were clearly shocked by the carnage and immense scale of the tragedy – he went about the business of checking the bodies inside and outside the plane with calm efficiency, delegating minor duties in a voice of quiet authority. And as he examined the air commodore's body, which had been thrown clear of the wreck, he had to confirm the searchers' initial fears. Although there was a severe gash on the dead man's head, his face was still recognizable to the doctor – who allowed himself a gasp of shock; for the face was that of the 39-year-old George Edward Alexander Edmund, Duke of Kent, youngest brother of the reigning King George VI. All doubt was dispelled on examination of the dead man's identity bracelet, which was inscribed: 'His Royal Highness The Duke of Kent, The Coppins, Iver, Buckinghamshire.' And although it did not seem important at the time, it was noted that his watch had stopped, presumably at the moment of the plane's impact with the ground.

As he concluded his tasks, supervising the covering of the most exposed bodies with their own parachutes, the elderly doctor shook his head with resignation. Although he did not know how many had been aboard the plane, it did appear that they had all perished, a few of them still lying, badly burned, inside the charred fabric of the overturned machine. He had not long reached that conclusion when one of the helpers, Police Constable Carter from Wick, suddenly exclaimed: 'Listen! I heard a human cry. I'm sure I did!' The others went quiet and listened hard; but they heard nothing but the sigh of the wind and the call of birds – and saw nothing but the rustling heather, even after they had spread out again to make a further search of the immediate area. Putting the alarm down as attributable to the policeman's imagination, which could well have been heightened by the nerve-racking high drama of the day's events, the doctor shook his head sadly again. There was little more he could do now but report to the authorities and help organize the removal of the bodies. This ardous task took place the following day, after Army personnel were brought in to guard the wreckage and the RAF flew a plane over to establish its precise location. All the bodies were conveyed over the difficult terrain to Wick – with the exception of the Duke's, which went first to Dunrobin Castle and was later removed to London.

A pilot who had risked his life during visits to many bomb-hit British towns, the Duke of Kent was once described by Winston Churchill as 'a gallant and handsome prince'. Known to friends and family affectionately as Georgie, the aircraft-loving Duke had a great deal to live for. Only seven weeks before the fatal Iceland-bound flight, he and his charming wife Marina – the Greek princess to whom he proposed in a lakeside chalet after borrowing the Prince of Wales' plane to fly to Slovenia – had celebrated the birth of their third son, Michael. Just after the birth, they had been visited by Queen Mary, who later reported in her diary that 'he looked so happy with his lovely wife and the dear baby'.

And Georgie was not only a patently happy husband and father; he was also delightedly in his element with the role that had been assigned to him in the RAF. Although as a young man he had spent ten years in the Royal Navy – initially based in Scotland, with naval intelligence in Rosyth – now, as Air Commodore, he was directly concerned with the welfare of RAF personnel, reporting to the department of the Inspector General on their living conditions and grievances. Always the most unconventional of the King's brothers, he would often arrive unannounced and unrecognized, perhaps driving his own car, on his visits to RAF home bases. But it was the longer trips he preferred. Loving flying as he did, he most relished his visits to far-flung bases, and indeed his last mission was to be concerned with the welfare of RAF men in Iceland which had been occupied by the British for over two years.

On the afternoon of 24 August, he said what was to be his last goodbye to Marina before setting out from London's Euston station on the overnight train to Inverness. The flight's designated departure point was nearby Invergordon, a naval base in the protected inlet of the Cromarty Firth. The Sunderland flying-boat that was to transport him was simultaneously flown there from its base at Oban, the crew aware only that something special was on. They must have felt immeasurably honoured to learn, late on the eve of the flight, that they were to be entrusted with such an important passenger. And indeed, they had been hand-picked for the mission. The pilot, Flight Lieutenant Frank Goyen, was a twenty-five-year-old Australian with an exceptional reputation and nearly 1,000 operational hours behind him. Seated beside him as first pilot would be another flyer of long and impressive experience, Wing Commander T.L. Mosley, Commanding Officer of 228 Squadron, and the crew that would back them up were all equally competent and reliable and included two more airforce pilots – Pilot Officer S.W. Smith, acting as second officer, and Pilot Officer G.R. Saunders acting as navigator. The crew numbered ten in all, every one a tried and trusted expert familiar with the admittedly rather cumbersome beast that was the Mark III Sunderland with its four Bristol Pegasus Radial engines. Daunting for some perhaps, but surely not for these exceptional men, every one of whom valued his life as much as the experience which was the key to his further enjoyment of it. So how could a flight so mightily endowed with long and wide professional ability have gone so drastically wrong after a duration of only about half-an-hour?

Certainly, the recent mild weather had broken and northern Scotland was blanketed with low cloud; but the waters of the Cromarty Firth were so calm that the Sunderland, carrying a full load of fuel for the long journey and depth-charges in case enemy submarines were spotted *en route*, had to make an unusually long run before cresting a wave big enough to punch it into the air. With the Duke comfortably ensconced in the wardroom in its belly, the heavy plane began to climb at the painfully slow rate of about 200 feet per minute, turning to port to follow the coastline. The idea presumably – though this is open to question – was to round the top of Scotland as much as possible over water, and to avoid short-cutting across the north-west Highlands where some high ground reached over 3,000 feet, presenting an obvious hazard to such a slow-climbing plane. But the most immediate hazard was a frustrating combination of vision-obscuring lowering cloud and mist. Roughly ten minutes into the flight, the skipper was heard to say 'Let's go down and have a look' and the plane descended to keep visual contact with the sea and the coastline on the left. But still more cloud appeared. As clearer weather was expected further north, around the Pentland Firth, some experts have been puzzled as to why the pilot did not simply push on to find it. Perhaps, it has been suggested, he was just trying to be a good host at this point – wanting to show his royal guest something of the north-east of Scotland – although the Duke had probably seen that part of the country before, having only the previous year visited Wick airfield to inspect RAF units there.

Accounts and opinions differ as to what the pilot did next. Considering the catastrophic consequence of what-ever it was that influenced his actions, it is often assumed that neither he nor his navigator can have been aware of a westward drift that was bringing the aircraft across the coast and near to inland high ground. Yet it is hard to accept that such a commonly-encountered factor in flying would not be acknowledged by a captain and crew of such vast experience, all of whom were doubtless monitoring every move like hawks. Nevertheless, apparently still descending, the plane crossed the coast just south of the Berriedale Water and, under the cloud and mist cover, the high land was coming up to meet it. It flew along the river valley – just avoiding the 2,000-foot summit of Meall Dhonuill, or Donald's Mount, – at the end of which was an unwelcome hill rising, at its western extreme, to an almost 1,000-foot-high bluff called Eagle's Rock. Then, as the pilot presumably saw the hill and battled with the controls to find more height – alas, too late – the Sunderland smashed to the ground and burst into the fatal fireball that consumed so many lives.

The sensational news of the fate of the Duke, the first royal to die on active duty, had an immediate impact not only at home, where public grief was unusually personal and sincere at the loss of such a popular figure; but also abroad, as the story was headlined all over the world. But nowhere was it more bitterly accepted than in the heart of his beloved family. Author Christopher Warwick poignantly recounts in his book, *George and Marina*, how those closest to the much-loved Georgie learned of the awful development:

That evening at Coppins, when the telephone rang, Marina had not long gone to her bedroom, intending to have an early night. Kate Fox, who had nursed the Duchess as a baby [in Greece] 36 years earlier and who had come out of retirement to nurse the now seven-week-old Prince Michael, took the call. Numb with shock, and perhaps wondering just how best to break the news, she slowly climbed the stairs. Hearing her, it is said that Marina immediately sensed catastrophe, and the moment Foxy opened the door, she cried out, 'It's George, isn't it?'

At Balmoral the King and Queen were having dinner with Harry and Alice, the Duke and Duchess of Gloucester, when the steward entered the dining room and whispered to the King that Sir Archibald Sinclair, Secretary of State for Air, was on the telephone and needed to speak to him urgently. When he rejoined his family, George VI was grim-faced and silent. 'The news,' he wrote, 'came as a great shock to me, & I had to break it to Elizabeth, & Harry & Alice who were staying with us ... We left Balmoral in the evening for London.'

When the King was called from the table, the Duchess of Gloucester's first thoughts were of Queen Mary – that something had happened to her. In fact the Queen Dowager had spent the day in active high spirits. During the morning she had driven over to Corsham Court, home of Lord Methuen, to attend a lecture and admire the picture gallery; had spent the rest of that wet afternoon at Badminton, putting photographs into her huge scarlet folio albums; and after tea had sat at needlework, while Lady Cynthia Colville, one of her ladies-in-waiting, read to her. News of Georgie's death was received shortly after dinner. 'I felt so stunned by the shock,' Queen Mary wrote in her diary, 'I could not believe it.' The following morning the Queen climbed into her famous old Daimler and drove to Coppins. When she arrived, she found Marina in a

pitifully desolate state; one moment sobbing uncontrol-
lably, the next staring blankly into space, utterly
motionless.

But there was to be still more drama on the remote
Scottish hillsides. From the body-count (there should have
been fifteen) it appeared that one person was still missing.
And indeed, twenty-two hours after the crash, came the
evidence that vindicated the 'imaginative' PC Carter's
keen hearing. One man, twenty-one-year-old rear gunner
Andrew Jack, had miraculously survived the crash, as the
tail turret of the Mark III Sunderland – normally
considered to be the most vulnerable part of such a plane –
had broken off almost intact. The next day, he
dramatically appeared three miles from the scene,
barefooted and dazed, his clothes in shreds, badly burned
about the face and body, at a lonely cottage where he just
managed to tell the lady of the house: 'I am an airman and
our plane has crashed. I am the sole survivor.' How did he
know that was the case? Despite his injuries, he had
searched the wreckage vainly for other survivors before
staggering off over the rough terrain towards the merciful
refuge of the cottage. He was looked after there until the
fortuitous arrival of Dr Kennedy who, passing that way
only by chance, was amazed not only to find a survivor
from the devastated plane but also to realize that he had
managed to walk so far over rough ground in such a bad
condition. Quickly removed to hospital in Lybster, the
young flight-sergeant made a good recovery.

Though he did recall a few details of the fateful flight –
such as the skipper Goyen's suggestion that they 'go
down and have a look' – this lucky son of a Grangemouth
dock foreman was never to be properly valued as the key
witness in the affair. Possibly because, despite an official
inquiry, the affair itself was oddly played down for many
years. Although it did eventually become a much-talked-
about mystery, the renewed interest came too late in the
day – Andrew Jack died in 1978 just before questions

began to be asked in earnest. But not before he had volunteered the opinion to his sister that he could never agree with the inquiry's finding that the crash had been caused by pilot error. Certainly, in the time-honoured tradition of all blame for such an accident being shouldered by the captain, the inquiry had not been disposed to give Flight Lieutenant Goyen much benefit of the doubt.

Sir Archibald Sinclair reported to the Commons on 7 October 1942, that the court of inquiry had found

> first, that the accident occurred because the aircraft was flown on a track other than that indicated in the flight plan given to the pilot, and at too low an altitude to clear the rising ground on the track; secondly, that the responsibility for this serious mistake in airmanship lies with the captain of the aircraft; thirdly, that the weather encountered should have presented no difficulties to an experienced pilot; fourthly, that the examination of the propellors showed that the engines were under power when the aircraft struck the ground, and fifthly, that all the occupants of the aircraft were on duty at the time of the accident.

If the aircraft had flown on a track 'other than that indicated in the flight plan' – and there were several ways of getting from Invergordon to Reykjavik – how can that be checked? Where is the flight plan now? It has apparently disappeared. Just one of many oddities discovered when, in the early eighties, Edinburgh writer and broadcaster Robin McWhirter decided to take up all the loose strings of the affair and try to tie them together. He quickly realized he was walking a path 'littered with inaccuracies' and found himself asking many key questions to which, for some reason, he could get no official answers. Such as: Why did the record book of 228 Squadron, Coastal Command, to which the flying-boat belonged, record 2 p.m. as the time of the crash when the plane took off a 1.10 p.m. and could not have been flying for much more than 30 minutes? (Indeed, the plane's clock had stopped at 1.30 p.m., while the time shown on the Duke's stopped watch was said to have indicated that the flight had lasted 32 minutes.) Why did *Hansard* record the date of the crash as 15 August, when the true date was ten days later? Why has all documentation pertaining to the official court of inquiry disappeared? Why do the Public Record Office, the RAF's Air Historical Branch and the Royal Archives at Windsor Castle all deny having the vital records relating to the death of the man who was fifth in line to the throne when he died? Why did the Queen's private secretary and keeper of the Windsor Archives state that he was 'not permitted to release the very few other documents which are of relevance'? Why, on the very day of the fatal flight, did pilot Goyan give Andrew Jack a signed photo of himself bearing the written message 'With memories of happier days'? Did the skipper perhaps know something that made him feel apprehensive about the forthcoming Iceland trip? A trip, incidentally, that Jack had made several times ...

Accepting that pilot error might not have been the cause, could there have been some sinister hand behind the 'accident' that had inevitably done considerable damage to British public morale? Not to put too fine a point on it: had an enemy agent tampered with the plane? There appeared to be no evidence and no way of proving such a thing but, paradoxically perhaps, in Lisbon of all places there was something a little more definite to support a theory of home-grown sabotage. In fact, recalled McWhirter, the German ambassador to Portugal, Baron Oswald von Hoyningen-Huene, had sent the following telegram to the German Foreign Minister Joachim von Ribbentrop on 5 December 1942:

> As the embassy has learned, confidentially, the death of the Duke of Kent has been discussed recently in the innermost circles of the British Club here. The gist of the talk being that an act of sabotage was involved. It is said that the Duke, like the Duke of Windsor, was sympathetic towards an understanding with Germany and so gradually

had become a problem for the Government clique. The people who were accompanying him were supposed to have expressed themselves along similar lines, so that getting them out of the way would also have been an advantage.

McWhirter was, however, unable to find any evidence to support this rather far-fetched contention and concluded that 'the British community in Lisbon was misinformed about those accompanying the Duke of Kent'.

Among the plethora of more technical, and less romantic, theories for the cause of the crash put forward by various writers and experts over the years have been the disorientating influence of magnetic rocks on the aircraft's compass (Ralph Barker: *Great Mysteries of the Air*) and the effect of down-draught on its altitude (Francis Thompson: *Murder and Mystery in the Highlands*). But it also has to be said that Skipper Goyen, although thought by many to have been unjustly maligned with the official pilot-error verdict, did not exactly receive the unqualified support of the RAF pilot who came along the next day to check the position of the wreckage from the air. This was the late Captain E.E. Fresson whose son Richard submitted the story of his flight for publication in letters page of *The Scotsman* in September 1985, after that newspaper had published McWhirter's searching questions on the affair. The pilot's log, as it was called, began on the same day as the crash ...

I happened to be on the Inverness/Kirkwall run that day and the Met Office reported bad weather along the route as far as the Pentland Firth, where conditions improved.

We flew north above the cloud at 4000 feet and found the Pentland Firth bathed in sunshine with the sea looking a deep emerald green. We departed from Kirkwall around one o'clock in the afternoon on the return trip and flew around the west side of Hoy across to Thurso in sunny weather. We caught up with the low cloud again at Thurso, when I turned off on the south-easterly course to bring the plane over Dunbeath on the Caithness coastline and which we passed over above cloud at 1.30 p.m.

At approximately the same time as we departed from Kirkwall, the [Duke's] Sunderland flying-boat took off from the Cromarty Firth ... climbed above the clouds and set course for the west side of Hoy, before changing course for the overseas flight to Reykjavik.

For some unknown reason, after being airborne for barely ten minutes, the captain was heard by the rear gunner over the intercom to say, 'Let's go down and have a look'. Knowing as he must have done that there was a very low ceiling on the first part of the trip, I never understood what possessed that captain to take such unnecessary risks. He only had to fly on course for another ten minutes and he would have had the whole of the Pentland Firth in view.

However, down they went and at about 200 feet they broke cloud to find themselves in a narrow valley, running parallel to the coastline, north of the small village of Berriedale. That valley extends roughly three miles northwards and at the end, the ground rises sharply up from near sea level to a thousand feet. With the poor visibility, the pilot evidently failed to see the sharply-rising ground in time. The aircraft clock found in the wreckage had stopped at half-past one, the time I was actually flying overhead and changing course for Inverness.

On the morning of August 26, I was informed through RAF Fighter Control at Drumossie about the accident. As the whereabouts of the wreckage was not accurately known, we were asked to keep a look-out on our flights north. I set out on a flight to North Ronaldsay via Kirkwall and I made for the Dunbeath area flying inland a few miles up the coast from Berriedale and over the same small valley where the Sunderland had evidently descended.

Suddenly we came on the wreckage at the top of the escarpment, strewn over a large area. The aircraft had evidently caught fire for the wreckage was still smoking. The fragmentation had evidently been severe, I descended to 100 feet and flew around. The four engines were scattered around the wreckage. The only recognisable part of the sea-plane was the rear gun-turret, rudder and tail-fin which had evidently broken away from the structure at the point of impact.

My radio officer and I could distinguish three or four bodies lying amongst the debris. It was obvious that the considerable amount of fuel on board had caught fire and had melted much of the light alloy wreckage. The position of the crash was some eight miles south-west of the village of Dunbeath and the altitude was around eight to nine hundred feet above sea level. The aircraft must have crashed in cloud.

After climbing to 2000 feet to obtain strong radio signals with Inverness, my radio officer tapped out a message to Inverness Control informing them that we had located the Sunderland and that, as far as we could tell, there were no survivors.

Three weeks after the disaster, on 14 September, King George VI drove from Balmoral to Berriedale, then made his way on foot towards the location of his brother's death. His party, which included the Duke of Sutherland, the chief constable of the county and several RAF officers, was led across the difficult terrain by a local gamekeeper, James Macewan, who had received the alarmed angler on the day of the crash – and passed on his alert to police headquarters at Wick. The King was also introduced to many of the other key players in the drama, including the shepherds David and Hugh Morrison and Dr Kennedy, who, as the searchers' spokesman, recounted to him the grim details of their discovery of the wreckage and bodies. And although the wreckage had by now been removed from the site, the royal guest was clearly moved by what evidence of the disaster remained to be seen. He later described his visit there as a 'pilgrimage' and wrote that 'the ground for 200 yds long & 100 yds wide had been scored and scorched by its trail & by flame. It hit one side of the slope, turned over in the air & slid down the other side on its back. The impact must have been terrific as the aircraft as an aircraft was unrecognisable when found'.

The heartbroken Marina could not bring herself to visit the site until several years later, and, perhaps thankfully, nature had by then done its healing work and there was little left to see of the path of devastation the King had described. Today, the spot is marked by a tall, simple cross atop a granite plinth bearing the names of those who died ... the only physical reminder of an unexplained tragedy whose cause, it seems, will be forever argued about.

Just as it was when McWhirter raised the subject in his *Scotsman* article timed to coincide with his 1985 radio programme, *The Crash of W-4026*. It did not just prompt the appearance of Captain Fresson's account. For days thereafter, the paper's letters page bubbled with theories, opinions and observations of varying quality, as the revitalized controversy took on an unprecedented intensity. Arguments between letter-writers bounced back and forth. Calculators were drawn. Rates of climb, distances and headings flown, the condition of the plane's instruments, the quality of the skipper's briefing, the time of the impact, the likelihood of sabotage, and even the possibility of the crew's performance being impaired by alcohol: all were gone into in the greatest of detail by expert and amateur alike. But in the end it seemed the baffled reader could reach only one conclusion: that precisely why the Duke of Kent's flying-boat had crashed remained a perplexing mystery, ever more unfathomable the more one considered the expertise and qualities of its crew.

One writer pointed out that such a crash was anything but rare during the war; that as many as 80 Sunderlands had been destroyed in and around Scotland, only two of them put down by enemy action. And 15 similar accidents had occurred in the area of the Duke's crash, 12 of them being fatal with a total of 77 lives lost. 'Hardly any of these,' wrote Malcolm Spaven, 'was attributed to technical causes; most were due directly to pilot or navigator error, leading to aircraft becoming hopelessly lost in cloud and flying into hills.'

What McWhirter would not yield to, however, was any suggestion that echoed the official inquiry's conclusion of 'a serious mistake in airmanship' being to blame. Having, in his original article, stressed the extreme unlikelihood of skipper Goyen making such an elementary error as failing to seek altitude in bad visibility, he countered with emphatic and final conviction:

> Frank Goyen was a cool, sober pilot with all six senses ticking over. That was why he and his crews survived so long among the dreadful statistics which Malcolm Spaven has listed.
>
> There is much more I could write about the crew of W-4026, but I will limit myself to one sentence: Whatever caused the tragedy at Eagle's Rock, it wasn't pilot error.

6   A Scream in the Night, 1945

Shrieking gulls wheel and glide in the bitter winds that sweep across the shoreline and power the huge waves that crash across the harbour mouth's protective piers like cascading fireworks. Elemental forces are still impressively at work around Aberdeen's ancient entrance from the North Sea where, on a chill December morning in 1945, Betty Hadden's severed left forearm was found washed up by such waves among the seaweed-coated stones on the south shore of the harbour's narrow navigation channel.

But the busy port's vital artery is probably a less sinister place today than it was then, when few people could have imagined the dramatic changes the oil industry would bring to the city's fortunes, based hitherto on the more traditional endeavours of agriculture and fishing. Nowadays, the trawlers have given way to a collective shuttle of brightly-coloured oil-supply vessels with names like *King Supplier* and *Oil Chieftain* that cleave through the channel's grey, undulating lifeblood to or from the black-gold fields with a cheeky, almost cheerful, confidence. There's a brasher edge to the city too, with the big oil tanks of Conoco and BP to the south, the high-rise sixties' flatblocks to the north.

It was a rather darker place in Betty Hadden's day, with the piratical vestiges of an older fishing-and-seafaring culture lingering on among the dockside bars and cafés in a network of seedy streets where now there are modern offices and service depots. For shiftless, glamour-seeking girls like Betty, the seductive old harbour area of Torry had a magnetic and masculine attraction, at a time of life when conventional entertainment wasn't enough: she would have been eighteen years old if she had lived a few more days. But her restless nature wouldn't wait for anything. Her home city wasn't exactly boring: it had plenty of dance-halls and picture houses where a girl could get a little second-hand taste of Hollywood stardust and excitement – nineteen cinemas, in fact; more than any other British city of comparable size. But Betty, who already had a variety of menial jobs behind her – waitress in a dockside café, fish-gutter, domestic servant, mill-hand – was more tempted by the first-hand escapism of real money and real excitement. And it seemed that the little brunette with the turned-down mouth and sulky eyes had discovered how to find it. A discovery that was to prove literally fatal.

But who killed Betty Hadden? In the beginning, it seemed that this elementary question would be quickly answered as the police made what the local press described as 'a brilliant start' to their enquiries on the case. For the most immediate mystery – to whom did the gruesome human remains found on the foreshore belong? – was solved within four hours. Yet, despite their flying start and prodigious and persistent follow-up efforts to run him to ground, the police ultimately failed to pin an identity on her killer, who remains to this day a 'person unknown'.

The first indication that something dreadful might have happened to a woman came with a scream that pierced through the early-morning darkness of 12 December. It rang out over the harbour area at around 2 a.m. and awakened many nearby people who, not entirely unaccustomed to late-night revelry and drunken disputes around Torry's quayside pubs, turned over in their beds and thought little more about it until subsequent press coverage and police enquiries sharpened their recall. Had that scream come from the throat of Betty Hadden as she struggled desperately with her killer? Nobody could ever be certain, but it seemed to fit in well with the sequence of events; for the second alarm, more shocking by far, was to come from the same area only about seven hours later that day.

While the cold Granite City started to get into its stride for what it assumed would be just another working Wednesday – the shops opening, the trams clanking up and down Union Street, the heavy horses and square-topped vans criss-crossing the thoroughfares to make their deliveries – old Alexander King was also up and about on his habitual morning pursuit: searching for driftwood on the south foreshore of the navigational channel, overlooked by a steep grassy embankment. When he saw the gleaming white object lying among the seaweedy pebbles and rocks, he stepped back warily for a moment, then gathered his courage to approach it again. Peering down to examine it, he gasped as he realized the object was a human forearm with the hand still attached and the fingers arched as if they had been scratching tensely at something or someone. There was a length of twine grannie-knotted around the wrist. Shocked and trembling, the 74-year-old retired cooper suddenly found some reserves of youthful energy as he hurried back up to the channel-side road, to call the police from the nearest telephone box.

First reactions to news of the discovery had a touch of battle-weariness about them; the war was just over, during which people had become accustomed to death and destruction, and this seemed like something similarly impersonal: the grisly relic, perhaps, of some distant sea battle or disaster. But when Detective-Superintendent John Westland, who was to lead the investigation, went to the mortuary to see the evidence for himself, he realized not only that it was rather too fresh for a wartime relic but also that there was something odd about it that required an expert eye. He called in police surgeon Dr Robert

Richards – who, after a preliminary examination, announced that it was the forearm of a young woman 'about 18 years old' who had been alive less than three days before. But it was his expert view on how it had been severed from the body that alerted police to the fact that this might not have been by accident. He shrugged aside colleagues' suggestions that the woman might simply have been drowned at sea and her drifting body accidentally dismembered by the propeller of a passing ship, and was emphatic about his own conclusion: that the arm had been quite deliberately cut off at the elbow, probably with a knife or a saw, or both.

All those present at this macabre scene looked at each other in the grim realization that what they were dealing with was evidence of a particularly calculated and cold-blooded murder. And as the arm was being routinely photographed – before being taken away for further examination to the forensic laboratories at Aberdeen University – Superintendent Westland issued an order which, he thought then, was based on only a slender and optimistic hope of quick identification: 'It should be fingerprinted as well, of course.'

His instinct was right; it signalled the 'brilliant start' acknowledged in the press. Already an entry in police files, the name Betty Hadden was found to match the prints from the arched, nicotine-stained fingers within a matter of hours. And a young detective received something of a shock when – as he was known to be looking for a girl of that name in connection with a minor offence at the old Castlehill Barracks – a laboratory colleague with a black sense of humour came to him, produced the forearm, and said: 'You wanted Betty Hadden, didn't you? Well, there you are!'

Immediately, the police launched a massive dragnet operation in the hope of making an equally quick arrest. Armed with long, probing 'graips' and working with small boats, wellington-booted officers turned over tons of tangle and flotsam as they scoured the boulder-strewn estuary for the rest of the body. Every ship in the harbour was checked from stem to stern and all those which had left in the previous few days were boarded by police at their next port of call. In a street-by-street comb-out of two square miles of the Torry district, officers spent hours of unpaid overtime going in and out of local houses removing washhand basins for forensic examination, through back gardens, down sewers, across wasteground, and into cellars, wash-houses and sheds, collecting every sample of blood they came across – but none matched Betty Hadden's. There was ox blood, fish blood, and even a dead pig became involved ...

To work out where the arm had originally entered the water, weather scientists from Aberdeen University were enlisted to co-operate with a special group of detectives assigned to the case. One of those detectives was John Nicol, who recalled some years later how 'the foreleg of a pig, representing the arm, was put into the water to test where the current would take it, and the winds and tides provided the answer.' Which was? The very point where the arm had been found! Clearly, if the murder had not actually been committed in the Torry district, disposal of at least part of it had taken place there. But from a ship or from dry land? That was only one of the vital questions which teased and challenged the police; but to which even speculative answers proved stubbornly elusive. With their frustration growing rapidly, and ship-checks proving fruitless, they appealed to residents of the district, and any motorists who had passed through it, to come forward with any information about anything unusual they had seen or heard on the night Betty was thought to have died: thus the scream-in-the-night stories that came first from an elderly woman, then from others who came forward. 'With the help of a volunteer policewoman, we even re-enacted the scene of a woman screaming down by the old Torry pier in the dead of night,' recalled Nicol, who later became an assistant chief constable of Grampian police. It helped – but only to strengthen the assumption of the time of the girl's death.

Meanwhile, Betty's mother, the widow of a shipyard worker, spoke uneasily about her daughter's shiftless life. 'More recently,' said Kate Hadden, 'she worked in fish yards but in her last two places she stayed only about three days.' She had not seen her daughter for nearly two weeks before her death, and she added that Betty had stayed away from home on previous occasions. Police began to build up a picture of the girl's aimless waterfront life: working here, working there, sleeping in unimaginable places, mixing with strangers by day and by night. They could not prove that the scream in the night was the last that was ever heard of her – or even that she died on that day, at that time – but they did manage to create a relatively reliable diary of late sightings of her.

On the previous Monday night, she was seen in the company of four girls opposite the town house; and on the same night a girl who knew her had seen her in Castle Street, walking arm-in-arm with two young naval ratings, one much taller than the other. The next day, she was seen first in the Torry area; then in the city centre, leaning against the wall of a shop 'eating buns and biscuits hungrily'; then back in the harbour area where 'she was trying to attract the attention of three sailors'. After which, she was never seen alive again. And try as they might, the police could make no progress in the search for her killer, whom they presumed to be a man – if only because of the clinical, clever, and quick butcher's technique that had been used to sever the arm.

Paul Harris, an Aberdonian author who has studied the case, voices one popular local view about Betty Hadden's fate when he says: 'I tend to go along with the school of thought that says she was simply picked up by some visiting sailors who had their way with her, perhaps over-violently, perhaps causing injury, then – suddenly afraid of repercussions – decided to shut her up for good by throwing her overboard in pieces to be fed to the fish.'

Indeed, despite its relatively short time in the water, the back of the hand had already been partially eaten by crabs; and there was something else interesting about it. The twine around the wrist had been bound so loosely that it seemed there had been a loop to it, inside which some kind of weight might had been placed – later accidentally slipping out. Along with various other pieces of potential evidence from the shore area of the arm's discovery – scraps of cloth, metal, and other materials – the twine was sent to the police laboratory at Nottingham for detailed examination by Dr H.S. Holden, the eminent forensic criminologist. It was found to be common binder twine of the kind used by tradesmen, farmers and shopkeepers, and yielded no new leads.

The arm, meanwhile, was taking on something of a life of its own. More experts had been called in to examine it, notably Professor Sydney Smith of Edinburgh University whose opinion, as one of Britain's foremost figures in forensic medicine, was highly valued – and backed up that of police surgeon Richards. The professor agreed with him that both a saw and a knife had almost certainly been used to dismember the arm and said that the size of the saw, and the pressure put on it, could be determined from the marks it made on the bone and from the point at which the last splinter broke off. Sir John Learmonth, another eminent authority – on the amputation of limbs – reported that by carefully reconstructing the body's dismemberment, he could establish the very position it was lying in when the 'operation' took place.

As time went on, and the police progress ground to a dispiriting halt, the limb became something of a celebrated object in the history of Scottish criminology. With the intention of preserving it for posterity, Professor R.D. Lockhart had it bottled, labelled and shelved in his anatomy department at Aberdeen University, and, thus packaged, it even made a macabre appearance – to the distress of some of the bow-tied guests – during a talk at the university given by Superintendent Westland. But several years after the anatomy professor's retirement, the arm was impulsively disposed of in a general clean-out of the department: a move which surprised many people, not least the professor himself. 'I am very sorry to learn that it has not been kept,' he told the press when he heard the news. 'If I had thought there was a possibility that they were not going to look after it, I would have brought it down to the Museum of Anthropology, where I am now curator.

So ignominiously vanished the last trace of the good-time girl who left two perplexing mysteries behind her: Where was the rest of her corpse? And who was her murderer? It is disturbing to conjecture that he might still be walking free in some far-off corner of the globe – or still living in the neighbourhood of Torry. 'Until his dying day,' said John Nicol, 'it remained a bitter disappointment to Superintendent Westland that the killer was never brought to justice and the case cleared up.'

Yet desperate police appeals to anyone anywhere who had access to the slightest piece of information potentially relevant to the case – however unimportant it might have seemed to them – did not bring forward Jack Webster, who was a schoolboy at the time: a time when the most popular musical act among the cheeky, short-trousered brigade was an irreverent blackly humorous rendering of *I Ain't Got No-body*. He is now a highly respected writer with the *Glasgow Herald*, and has latterly wondered if he might have been able to help the police to trace the murderer.

In his early fascination with newspapers and avid study of their treatment of such sensational tales, he remembers being riveted to the unfolding story in the *Aberdeen Evening Express*. He noted especially a line in one report that said Betty Hadden had close friends in the city's Froghall district, and another line that a youth had been known to carry messages to her there. 'I knew I was not that youth,' he writes in his autobiography, *A Grain of Truth*, 'though the description was similar; but from the hazy recollection of the name on the envelope, I had carried a note to someone who could have been Betty Hadden or a friend of hers who had an address in Froghall. The police were anxious to trace sailors and I had a clear picture of the one [who had given him the note] at Holburn Junction.'

How had this come about?

At the corner of Holburn Junction, my friend Alastair Crombie and I were distracted by a call from a doorway. It was a sailor asking if we would care to earn a couple of bob by delivering a message. We would have to take a letter to a certain house, wait to see if there was a reply, and bring it back to the same place at a given time.

Swayed by the prospect of earning two bob instead of spending it, we agreed and set out for a district which had a mixed reputation: Froghall. It was a slum-clearance district, it seemed, but even then deteriorating into the sort of condition from which the inhabitants had so recently moved. We climbed the communal staircase, gripped by a sleazy excitement in this rather sinister setting ... Nervously, we knocked on the door which was opened by a woman of brittle appearance who took the letter and disappeared inside. From the doorway, a couple of fourteen-year-olds, slightly apprehensive, could see and hear the revelry of a carefree household. The war was over and it was pub-closing time as drunken servicemen lolled in chairs with women on their knees, exposing legs and thighs and goodness knows what. The woman who took the note returned to say that there would be no reply, so we left and hurried back to Holburn Junction for the appointed hour.

The sailor, a smallish, dark, stocky fellow, was already there waiting. We gave him the news and never saw him again ...

Could that have been a significant incident? Jack Webster admits that he just doesn't know, 'but Alastair and I sat on our secret, nervously protecting ourselves with silence [to avoid the risk of severe discipline at school] ... a silence maintained while sailors on boats were followed to the ends of the earth.'

Certainly, as recalled by John Nicol, there was a chance that a sailor was the culprit but 'we got no results after checking all ships which had sailed from Aberdeen'. He preferred to believe, in any case, that the killer was a local man. 'A man in Torry was our chief suspect, but we did not have enough evidence against him.'

Despite Paul Harris's feeling that Hadden was thrown overboard from a visiting ship, many other writers speculating about the case seem to have agreed with Nicol; to have formed a general consensus that the killer lived (and lives still?) locally. Webster himself claims:

> The killer of Betty Hadden had probably disposed of the body in a trunk but was unable to tuck in the surplus arm. So he sawed it off and carelessly disposed of it in the river. There were those who believed that the murderer was a local person who knew the lie of the land, a quiet inhabitant of Torry who continued perhaps to live out his life with an air of respectability.

And Peter Piper wrote in the *Scottish Sunday Express*:

> Betty Hadden, shiftless and haphazard as she was, was not a 'pick-up girl' in the accepted sense of that phrase. I feel convinced that on the night of December 11 she met someone ruthless and brutal and savage enough to attempt by force to overcome her. She fought against this man and died. And I believe, too, that this man lived in Torry or nearby, or at least had access to some building there where he dismembered the body.

All of which gives rise to an uncomfortable thought. If Betty Hadden's body had indeed been squashed into a trunk, and if her killer were indeed a local man, where is that trunk now? Was it also confined to the deep? If not, it seems inconceivable that the murderer, presumably shocked by the boomerang-like return of the once-weighted arm, would have taken another similar – and even greater – risk by returning to the water to dispose of the trunk and the butchered body. The idea is undoubtedly a ghastly one, but no less ghastly than the whole macabre tale itself: could the unrecovered remains of the sulky good-time girl still be awaiting discovery – perhaps under the lawn of someone's respectable back garden – in the vicinity of the waterfront world where she met her untimely, nightmarish death?

Time might ultimately tell; and then again, it might not ...

7   Sealed Lips, 1960

At first sight, it seemed just like a case of a domestic argument that had gone tragically over the top. In court, Henry Daniels, a 61-year-old roofer, didn't deny that on the Saturday afternoon in question he had had a row with his wife because he had come home late from work – but he claimed he had not even risen from his chair and did deny, most emphatically, that he had violently assaulted her in the late evening and consequently caused her death.

Domestic rows were nothing new in a post-war Glasgow blighted by the pressures of urban deprivation and overcrowding, and neighbours who witnessed or overheard them would usually consider them worth little more than a shrug of the shoulders. Such a joyless home environment could – when combined with the difficulties of scraping a living from a harsh world of declining industry, with little extra to spend on leisure – make people feel pent-up and quickly irritable. But home-life at Castlemilk, where Daniels and his wife Elizabeth had gone to live, was supposed to be different.

The city had recently become sensitive to outsiders' comments on its slum problems and was trying to solve them with schemes like this – new homes away from the centre, on the south side of the river Clyde, with nice bathrooms and kitchens into which yesterday's deprived families could be decanted to build themselves a better tomorrow. Today, the area has declined again and, looking at it, few people would say it offered much relief with its grey over-tight mix of shoulder-to-shoulder blocks and occasional high-rise towers, offset only by a few community improvement schemes. But for the Daniels it was, at the time, a brave and refreshing new world and, indeed, the husband claimed that their old world hadn't been so bad either: their relationship throughout their 35-year-long marriage, he said, had been 'good'.

Nevertheless, it could not be denied that something terrible had happened to bring about a disastrous end to that relationship in the couple's Castlemilk house on the evening of Saturday, 18 June 1960 ... when neighbours heard sounds of a commotion coming from their house: there were 'thuds', as if someone were jumping up and down, and punching and slapping noises. And the consequence of all this was coolly announced in a couple of small paragraphs in the following Thursday's *Glasgow Herald*. The report's position in the paper, tucked away between what were obviously perceived as the much more important stories of the previous day – the Queen visits the Royal Highland Show, seven killed in factory explosion at Bishopton – seemed to suggest that it was only to be regarded as yet another domestic row gone wrong. A case of private tragedy that would be opened, shut, and quickly forgotten ...

MURDER CHARGE
IN GLASGOW

Henry Daniels (61), a Glasgow man, was charged yesterday in Glasgow Central Police Court with the murder of his wife. He was ordered by the Stipendiary Magistrate to be remitted to the Sheriff Court and committed to prison for four days for examination.

Officers of the CID were called to a home at 5 Lenihall Terrace, Castlemilk, on Saturday after a woman was found with head wounds. She died in hospital on Monday.

It was not to be as simple as that, however. When Daniels eventually appeared in the High Court on a reduced charge of the culpable homicide of his wife by 'knocking her to the floor and striking her repeatedly on the face and head with his fists, whereby she was so seriously injured that she died', he fervently denied the charge – and the only other person who could cast light on the matter felt himself unable to do so. The moral dilemma of Roman Catholic priest Jeremiah O'Flynn was to make this trial unique in British legal history.

As the local parish priest, he had been called to the scene of the crime by a neighbour who went to investigate the violent sounds coming from the Daniels' house – to find the door open and Mrs Daniels lying in the hallway, covered in blood. When he arrived, some twelve minutes before the police, the priest realized that the woman was probaby fatally injured, although she was still conscious and reasonably coherent. He immediately saw it as his duty to administer to her the Last Rites and to take her last Confession – during which she confided to him the cause of her injuries. The unsuspecting priest thus became a potentially key witness in the affair and a focus of considerable legal debate.

While some police-officers tracked down the victim's 'missing' husband to arrest him within hours, others, who were engaged in the collation of evidence – statements from neighbours, signs of a struggle in the house but no sign of a forced entry – also called on Father O'Flynn to make a statement: which he did, briefly mentioning only the reason for, and time of, his arrival and what he did thereafter. But as all the available evidence was weighed and assessed, including the result of forensic tests that found Daniels' heavy boots to have minute traces of blood on them, it was quickly realized that the essential substance of the words Father O'Flynn had heard from Mrs Daniels would constitute vital evidence in the resolution of the case.

The priest was soon equally aware of his pivotal position, especially in the light of the fact made clear to him that, without his evidence, the case for the Crown would fall considerably short of having the proof beyond reasonable doubt required to effect a conviction. And so began his dilemma. Should he, could he – even in the interests of justice and truth – reveal what Mrs Daniels had said to him under the inviolable Seal of the Confessional? So important did the quandary become to him that he felt obliged to consult not only the Archbishop of Glasgow, but also the Pope himself. And the priest maintained later that his inclination not to tell had been vindicated by his superiors. He thus became determined that his lips would remained sealed and that the secret information imparted to him by Mrs Daniels would go with him to the grave, despite the fact that he would probably be asked to divulge it when he appeared as a Crown witness at a High Court trial of extreme gravity.

Meanwhile, Mr Daniels' son had asked Joseph Beltrami, one of Scotland's most celebrated criminal defence lawyers, to represent his father. The lawyer took on this challenging brief with alacrity and immediately went to speak to the accused in prison – where he vehemently denied any part in the assault on his wife. After the serving of the indictment – with the final charge, list of witnesses and productions – on both himself and his new client, Beltrami also went to see Father O'Flynn twice at his chapel house in Castlemilk. Their first meeting was notable for the priest's firm statement of his resolve to remain silent, but at the second – recalls Beltrami in his book, *The Defender* –

> I could see Father O'Flynn was almost at the point of collapse. He reiterated that he would not divulge what he had been told, despite the possible consequences. He had visions of being held in contempt of court and possibly being sent to prison because of this. The Crown had made it clear how vital his evidence might be in the case, and had advised him that they would try to compel him to answer their questions. For my part, I told him there would almost certainly be a legal debate on this point and that the defence would formulate objections to his answering when the Crown sought to make him break his seal of confession.
>
> I felt that, after the matter had been properly ventilated

before the trial judge, Father O'Flynn would almost certainly be advised that he need not answer. He was grateful for my reassurance, but we both realised that we were embarking on novel legal ground, as there was no precedent in Britain for such a situation. That being so, one could not be certain as to the outcome. But it was clear to me that this priest would go to prison rather than break the Seal …

When the case came to court in mid-September of the same year, Father O'Flynn was indeed called by the Crown in the course of the first day's evidence, and the crowded court was hushed as he was asked by the advocate-depute if he had been told by the dying woman how she had come by her injuries and who had caused them. He replied: 'Yes.'

'And what did she say?'

'It is in the nature of a professional [or confessional] secret,' he responded, implying that, because of his vocation, he was not empowered to make public this information. He was bound by the 'strictest obligation' not to reveal anything said to him in confession. 'I can therefore say nothing about what passed between Mrs Daniels and me … The laity entrust us, as spiritual advisers and consultants, with many things they would not tell to other people.'

After Father O'Flynn had explained the irrevocable confidentiality of the Confessional Seal in greater detail, the advocate-depute warned him: 'This is a serious charge of culpable homicide.' At which point, the jury was asked to retire while the defence came forward to prompt a legal debate later described by Beltrami as 'enthralling', particularly because of the lack of precedent and therefore guidance from an earlier ruling. After listening to this intently, the trial judge, Lord Patrick turned to address the priest: 'I am not going to force you to say anything that was said in confession, but anything that was not said in confession, you are bound – in the interests of justice – to tell the court.'

It is here that the reported accounts of the trial make an interesting divergence. In his book, Mr Beltrami writes that, thereafter, 'a greatly relieved Father O'Flynn left the witness box – and the Crown case was thus stripped of evidence which might have been of value to either side, and no one but the priest knew which'. The *Glasgow Herald* report of 17 September mentions no sequel, but *The Scotsman* report of the same day goes on to add: 'Father O'Flynn said that, when he went into the house ... Mrs Daniels told him: "He beat me".'

Now retired and living in Ireland, Father O'Flynn still prefers to keep his lips sealed. But on the face of it, these would seem to have been key words which, if said, were presumably voiced outwith the confessional. But lawyer Beltrami denies that they were ever said – 'I was there!' – adding that this must have been simply a case of misreporting. 'If such words had been said, there would have been very little point in the whole legal debate.' And yet ... couldn't 'he', despite its undeniable ring of familiarity, have meant anybody? As Mr Beltrami wrote in conclusion to his own account: 'For all the court knew, Mrs Daniels might have indicated [to the priest] that a complete stranger had been responsible, and that he might have entered the house after knocking on the door.'

That was certainly the implication in Mr Daniel's defence of himself. Under questioning, he admitted that he and his wife had argued for about twenty minutes on the Saturday in question, but claimed he had never struck her or assaulted her in any way. When she was crying later that day, he thought it was because of a headache. 'This sort of thing had been happening for years,' he added. She frequently complained of headaches and had poor health; but they had been married since 1925 and had always had 'good relations'.

The defence did not lead any evidence on the second and last day of the trial but argued strongly that the Crown case could not be proved to the necessary standard ... 'the standard,' according to Beltrami, 'that is very properly placed on the Crown in all criminal charges in this country'. But the jury seemed a trifle unsure. After retiring for four minutes, they said they wished for more information and the court was resumed for about two minutes, during which Lord Patrick advised them that they could return a majority verdict on any one of the three choices possible under Scots law: guilty, not guilty, or not proven.

This last is one of the unhappiest features of a legal system that has otherwise good reason to be proud of itself. It is a hangover from the days when it was the only alternative to guilty and therefore meant an unequivocal not guilty. Today, however, it is described by a highly-placed legal officer as 'the soft option for a less-than-decisive jury' and, although it certainly allows the accused to walk free, he or she might never feel completely cleansed by it. It was this verdict that the jury in his case handed down to Henry Daniels after two hours and eight minutes of deliberation.

The defence lawyers had good reason to be satisfied, however, having not only succeeded in effecting their man's release but also in establishing that which had not been available to guide them – an important legal precedent which seemed unlikely to be overturned in the future. But Henry Daniels did not live to enjoy his freedom for very much longer. He died of natural causes about a year later, though not before he had told the press: 'The death of my wife was a deep loss to me. I just don't know how she was injured.'

It follows that Mrs Daniels' husband was absent at the time of the assault; that she was alone in the house and therefore vulnerable to the kind of random crime that still, and even increasingly, blights such undefended neighbourhoods. The stranger's knock at the door; the plausible story achieving easy entry; then the violent attack. Coming hard on the heels of a domestic row, such an attack could prompt a convenient assumption and it is easy to see how the husband could have become the chief suspect. But he could, equally easily, have been the victim of a cruel coincidence. It now seems unlikely that we shall ever know the real attacker; that we shall ever be able to put a name to the 'he' allegedly referred to by Mrs Daniels. For the only person who knows for sure is morally bound to take that name to the grave ... and is quite determined to do so.

8   Blood Money, 1968

Apart from the howling of the chill North Atlantic winds that sweep across its bleak, treeless moors, it is normally a very quiet place, the island of Lewis. Survival and social interdependence being high priorities with its hardy people who have quite enough trouble from the elements, there is little time for hostility among neighbours. A murder is thus a very rare occurrence in their far-flung north-western fastness and when it happens, it is met with shock and disbelief. In fact, there have been only two in living memory – in 1938, when an islander was charged with killing his wife but escaped execution by being certified insane; and in 1968, when the close-knit island community was appalled at the brutal murder of an old woman in the tiny west-coast village of Brue, in Barvas parish about twelve miles from Stornoway.

Who was responsible for the second murder? That is the mystery that has bewildered many islanders since a young weaver walked free from the High Court at Inverness three months after the discovery of 80-year-old Mary Mackenzie's body on a mid-November morning. A neighbour, crofter Angus Maclean, had become suspicious when he noticed that her bedroom curtains, normally drawn and pinned only at the bottom to form a V-shape because she was too small to reach up further, were completely closed. Finding the kitchen door unlocked, he entered the old lady's little house and called out her name repeatedly. But there was no response – so he ventured into the bedroom to be confronted by a macabre scene. Surrounded by pieces of torn newspaper – it was generally known that the rather eccentric old lady kept considerable sums of money wrapped up in bundles of such paper – Miss Mackenzie was lying on the floor in a pool of blood. Her nightdress and stockings were bloodstained, there were lacerations on her head, and her hands were folded across her breast. It appeared that her feet had been moved, describing an arc in the blood. And a broken alarm clock was found beside her, with its hands stopped at 5.55, although Mr Maclean knew that one of her odd habits was to keep the clock running two hours fast.

At 9.15 on the following Tuesday night, CID officers led by Detective Superintendent Robert Brown of Glasgow, entered the nearby home of 21-year-old weaver George Macleod and arrested him. Soon charged with murder at Stornoway Sheriff Court, he was taken to Stornoway airport by police officers to board the flight for Inverness, where he was to be held, until his High Court trial, at Porterfield Prison. That was when the shock that had kept the island talking since the body's discovery turned into stunned disbelief. Macleod was one of a respectable family of four sons and three daughters who, living less than a hundred yards from Mary Mackenzie's house, knew the old lady well. In the same court where he was accused of striking her repeatedly on the head with an unknown instrument and robbing her of a sum of money unknown – and a handkerchief – he was also described by witnesses as 'a quiet lad' and 'a likeable and well-behaved boy'. And not surprisingly perhaps, his father Donald characterized him in the witness-stand as 'a good-hearted fellow'.

When the long and complicated five-and-a-half day trial got under way before the Lord Justice Clerk, Lord Grant, the apparent shattering of the innocence of island life seemed to capture the public imagination: there were queues of people lining up for the sessions, and on the last day as many as two hundred were turned away. But if they had hoped to hear evidence that would inject clarity and definition into the case, they were to be disappointed. What they heard was a confusing chain of circumstantial facts and scenarios that could be broken, claimed the defence, 'link by link'. Paradoxically, it was perhaps an indication of the inherent weakness of the Crown's case that there were no fewer than eighty prosecution witnesses cited to appear, while only six were scheduled to be put forward by the defence, led by Lionel Daiches QC, the formidable advocate once described – by writer and broadcaster Colin Bell – as 'the undisputed master of the final speech to the jury, the extravagant display of learning, wit and language which can occasionally acquit a man in the teeth of all the evidence ... in whose hands a minor discrepancy in the evidence becomes a monstrous chasm of injustice through which the Crown will pass only at our peril'.

As the trial went on, before a jury of seven men and eight women, it began to look like a classic case for the Daiches treatment. While conceding that the evidence against Macleod was largely circumstantial, Advocate-Depute John McCluskey QC sought, through witnesses, to demonstrate that all the elements added up to the sum of guilty.

It appeared that the murder – the obvious motive for which was robbery – had taken place in the early hours of Friday 15 November. Dr Ian Murray said he examined Miss Mackenzie, who had been his patient, at about noon that day and estimated that she had died between six and twelve hours earlier, after being bludgeoned by an instrument that was 'not very sharp or very heavy ... it would have had an edge of some kind, but not a sharp edge'. And Dr Edgar Rentoul, a Glasgow University lecturer in forensic medicine who carried out a post-mortem on the body, said she died from multiple lacerations of the scalp, fractures of the skull, and concussion. In his opinion, the 'cruel and savage' attack was probably carried out with a blunt object 'such as an iron bar, a stone, or even a boot'. There was talk of a crow-bar that had been seen in the possession of Macleod's friend Donald Matheson around the time of the murder, and it was produced as an exhibit in court. But in reply to Mr Daiches, Matheson claimed the crow-bar had remained in a cupboard at his home on the night of 14 November and all the following day.

Dolina MacDonald, a neighbour of both Macleod and the murdered woman, told the court she had been disturbed around the presumed time of the killing by a knock on her window – and the voice of Macleod calling her name. She called out: 'What are you doing here at this time of night?' And they exchanged comments about the time: she said it was two in the morning, and as she saw him illuminate his watch with the aid of a burning cigarette, he claimed it was going on for midnight. 'I told him to go home and he said he was sorry.' When, after learning of Miss Mackenzie's murder, she saw spots of blood on the window, she reported the incident to the police. But when Daiches pointed out that forensic scientists had established that the blood on the window was that of a hen, she responded: 'Yes, I know that now.'

Detective-Inspector James Junor read a statement given by Macleod during an interview at Stornoway police station, in which the accused claimed he had been drinking with friends until 1.30 on the morning in question and then 'went straight home. I was not near any other place that night. I haven't been in old Mary's house for a month'. But then there was the small matter of the suitcase found in his house …

At the police station, Macleod had been invited to unlock it, and did so with a key on a ring taken from his pocket. The case contained a number of items, including a handkerchief and £45 in an envelope. This money, it was alleged, included 23 single £1 notes of the British Linen Bank, seven of them bearing the serial number T/4. Earlier, it had been stated that £100 in new British Linen notes of the T/4 series had been issued to old age pensioners in the area, whereas the accused was paid for his weaving work in notes of the Bank of Scotland and Bank of England. And PC John Fraser, questioned by Mr McCluskey, agreed that his inquiries among a cross-section of the community, in search of British Linen Bank notes bearing that serial number, had been less than successful.

The jury also heard that a National Commercial Bank £1 note allegedly found in the suitcase had a piece missing from it, and two pieces of a banknote found at the dead woman's home had, according to the police, fitted the gap perfectly. The joining-up of the jigsaw was demonstrated to the jury with a series of photographs, but Daiches tackled this challenging exercise laterally. 'Was there anything found on Macleod or his clothing to indicate that he had been in that house?' he asked the first policeman delivering this evidence – who replied: 'As far as I am aware, no, sir.' And from the policeman in charge of the photographs – Detective-Inspector Osborne Butler, of the Identification Bureau, City of Glasgow Police – the admission was extracted that he had been unable to find one single, whole, identifiable fingerprint there. A strand of hair found clutched in Miss Mackenzie's hand had promised to be an important clue, but on examination it had not come from George Macleod and was similar in texture and colour to her own.

One of the key planks of the prosecution's case was George Macleod's apparently urgent need for money. Social Security inspector Alistair Mackenzie pointed out that, while in the two previous years Macleod had sent in his National Insurance stamp card to them after only one reminder, for the year in question he had needed two reminders. And clerical officer Mary Morrison said that the due sum of £47 19s was paid on 15 November all in single notes ...

The Advocate-Depute saw this 'sudden acquisition of wealth', on the morning after Miss Mackenzie's death, as 'significant'. And in his closing speech, he also pointed out not only that robbery had been the only possible motive for the crime but that the old lady's assailant must have been someone she knew and recognized ...

In Macleod's defence, however, Daiches pointed out that he had no record of violence and suggested that the wrong man had been charged. He said the prosecution's deductions made 'a chain strung out by fibres of the imagination which could be blown away by a breath of air'. There was nothing to connect George Macleod with the murder house or the murder itself. He referred to several of the items of evidence on which the prosecution case depended – the crow-bar, the hair clutched in the victim's hand, the handkerchief, the hen's blood on the neighbour's window – and asserted that none of them had ultimately anything to do with the case. 'As one looks at the Crown case, one sees it melting away before one's eyes,' he said. 'It just doesn't add up.'

And caution was the judge's watchword. In his summing up to the jury, which lasted one-and-a-half hours, Lord Grant warned of the dangers of speculation and suspicion, reminding them of the circumstantial nature of the Crown evidence. Had guilt beyond reasonable doubt been established? The onus on the Crown to prove this was a heavy one. The questions of robbery and murder in the case were very much inter-related. If it had not been ascertained that Macleod had robbed Miss Mackenzie, the jury could not bring a guilty verdict. The question for its members was whether the evidence as a whole established guilt ... and, unless Macleod was guilty of the whole charge, he was not guilty at all.

Eighty minutes of tension followed – later described by George Macleod as 'the longest wait I have had in my life' – then, as the jury returned to announce its unanimous 'not proven' verdict, spontaneous applause broke out from the packed public gallery. Macleod himself took the news quietly and calmly, but more applause filled the courtroom as Lord Grant discharged the 21-year-old weaver. Twice, a court official had to rise and shout for silence as the longest trial of its kind to be held in Inverness came to an undignified close.

Outside the courtroom, surrounded by back-slapping friends and relatives congratulating him in Gaelic, a relieved Macleod told reporters about the 'terrible strain' he had been under. 'I was feeling weak sometimes during the trial, knowing that I had nothing to do with it and yet people were coming out with evidence against me. I was wondering why on earth all this was happening to me when I had nothing to do with it.' He revealed that, on the Saturday night after Miss Mackenzie's death, he had attended a wake for her in the village. 'I was feeling terrible to hear about her death, and it was even more terrible to be charged with her murder after having been at her wake.'

'Not proven' being a uniquely Scottish verdict that lacks the definite, thoroughly cleansing conclusion of 'not guilty', he was asked if he felt completely satisfied with the jury's decision. 'I'm not worried about the verdict,' he said, 'so long as I'm free ... I'm feeling fine now and I'm going back to the weaving.' Simultaneously, back in Brue – across the road from where Miss Mackenzie lived – his mother broke down and wept when she heard the jury's decision. 'This is wonderful news,' she said. 'It is a tremendous relief to us all and an answer to our prayers. I am glad it is all over ... George is still a young lad and I hope he will soon get over this terrible experience.'

So who was the killer of Mary Mackenzie? One of Lionel Daiches' witnesses, who was dubbed the Red Herring, obviously had suspicions about a dark stranger who appeared in Barvas on the night of the murder – but, as the evidence had no direct relevance to the Macleod case, the matter was passed over without further development. Nevertheless, to garage proprietor Ian Macdonald there seemed something sinister about the mysterious caller who approached him as he was working late on a difficult job at about midnight on 14-15 November. The man – black-haired, about 26 years old, roughly 5 ft 6 in tall, wearing a grey-and-black checked coat and grey trousers – asked for a gallon of petrol to be put in a carrying can.

'He was not a local man,' the garage proprietor told the court. 'He sounded more like an Englishman than a Lewis man. He walked off in a westerly direction towards Brue Road junction [also the direction to Mary Mackenzie's house] and I saw him again at about 1 a.m. or 1.30 a.m. with a Ford van. It had windows in the sides.' The man then asked him for four gallons of petrol, at which point Mr Macdonald said he noticed some airline travel bags in the back of the van – and that the last two letters on the van's registration plate were SB. He then paid with paper money and was given change – although, in answer to Mr Daiches, the garage man said the police had made no examination of the notes in his cash register after he had mentioned the matter to them.

He had done this on the following Saturday, when he heard of possible foul play in connection with Miss Mackenzie's death. And on that same day, he had seen the van again, being driven in the Stornoway direction, although he had not noticed the driver. He had also mentioned this to the police, he told the court, but had heard nothing further from them.

Today, Ian Macdonald talks disparagingly of the trial – 'all I remember was parading up and down a corridor in Inverness as the last but one witness to be called' – and sympathetically about George Macleod. 'He's been at sea ever since and managed to keep his head very well.' But what of the dark stranger? Macdonald clearly still has his suspicions. 'I remember that, when he first asked for petrol, he had difficulty scraping up the money to pay for it; in fact, I don't think he even managed to find enough for a gallon. Then, when he returned, he seemed to have plenty of paper money. I can't now remember exactly what kind of notes they were, but I thought it all very odd, especially as the man was a complete stranger to me. What was he doing here at that time in the morning? For some reason, I had the impression that he was an RAF man; but after I caught that glimpse of his van on the Saturday, I never saw him again.'

9   Bible John's Fatal Charm, 1968

Surprising as it may seem, his fantasies, interests and
practices do not always make religion unacceptable to him,
and sometimes there is not only a declared interest in it but
he may be a church-attender. He can also be sanctimo-
nious and sometimes quote scripture ... He may describe
opposing forces warring within him, referring to them as
Good and Evil or God and the Devil.

Just like Bible John?
In his study of *The Sadistic Murderer*, the late Dr Robert P.
Brittain, eminent psychiatrist and lecturer in forensic
medicine, also suggested that, while some sadistic sexual
offenders might have characteristics that support the
average preconception – brutish, of low intelligence,
aggressive, insensitive, rough, crude, vulgar – 'the
majority appear to be much like other people'.
Just like Bible John?
Yes and no. This particular monster, who is believed to
have murdered three women in relatively quick succession in the late sixties after nights out at Glasgow's
Barrowland Ballroom, now a pop concert hall, certainly
appeared to be quite the opposite of brutish – if we are to
believe the description we have of him, which has been
called one of the most precise in Scottish police history.
But he was not, in the context of his operating
environment, quite 'like other people' either. Paradoxically perhaps, the man thought to be Bible John stood out
in the raucous Glasgow dance-hall crowd because of his
very 'respectability'.

The sister of one of his presumed victims said simply: 'He was not the Barrowland type.' The Barrowland type was loud-mouthed, aggressive, fashionably long-haired, and probably much the worse for the large quantity of drink he had consumed before launching himself into the dance-hall's seething mass of gyrating bodies. 'John' was different because he didn't drink or smoke; his reddish-brown hair was unfashionably short and neatly trimmed; he was tall and rather delicately handsome, polite and well-spoken with a soft Glasgow accent; and although he was in his late twenties and did wear reasonably modern clothes such as Italian-style suits and high-sided boots, the general impression he gave was of a well-brought-up professional or military type with considerable charm. Altogether, something of a ladies' man ...

His interests apparently included golf and religion, and it remains ironic and deeply puzzling that such a clear description – which included details like a slight overlapping of one front tooth across another – should not have delivered the man into the hands of one of Britain's most hardened police forces which, with much less to go on, has tracked down many a major criminal working in much more covert circumstances than a dance-hall packed with hundreds of potential witnesses.

Part of the problem was, however, that many of these people should not have been there in the first place: they were fugitives from shaky marriages, or just less-than-faithful boyfriends or girlfriends looking for a little 'something on the side'. So – even if they could conceivably help – they were reluctant to come forward for fear of having to go public and being found out by their usual partners.

At first, too, there was no reason to believe that a triple-murderer was at large. In a city that has always had more than its share of violent crime, the occasional case of a late-night quarrel going fatally over the top was just one of those unfortunate things that would soon become no more than a vague memory. Nevertheless, the shock was real enough when, on a raw February morning in 1968, Maurice Goodman walked towards his car lock-up in a quiet lane in Langside and discovered to his horror the dead and naked body of ...

Victim No. 1

The previous Thursday evening, vivacious 25-year-old nurse Patricia Docker had asked her parents, with whom she was living at Langside, if they would look after her four-year-old son – from a broken marriage – while she went out dancing to the Majestic Ballroom. They were happy to do so, for she was a hard-working lass who deserved a little relaxation. But they never saw her alive again. Exhaustive police enquiries proved, after many wasted days of checking out false leads from that establishment, that she had not been there at all. She had been at the Barrowland Ballroom. And by this time, memories had dimmed or were consciously made to dim – for Thursday was the most 'secret' night of the week for over-25 dancers who preferred not to reveal their presence there.

Although the police did offer to preserve anonymity, they qualified this by saying that the offer would have to be withdrawn if any useful material evidence were forthcoming. Not surprisingly, the only response they got was complete silence.

Faced with the dismal prospect of failure, the police could only go over the known ground again and surmise that Pat Docker had been the victim of someone who had taken her home from the dancing, for her body had been found very near to her parents' house. From that point, there were certain things they knew: she had been strangled, suggesting a certain premeditation; she had been menstruating and there was no clear evidence of sexual assault; there was no sign of her clothes, as if her killer had taken some trouble to remove and conceal them; and a neighbour had reported hearing a female cry of

'Leave me alone!' the night before the body was found.

The nurse's estranged husband, an RAF man based at Digby, Lincolnshire, was checked out. Although he had been on leave in Scotland at the time, his parents said he had been at their home in faraway East Lothian on the night of the murder, and in St Andrews the following day. He was traced there to be informed of his wife's death and agreed to go to Glasgow to confirm identification of her; but he could offer no clue to her recent activities since he had not seen her for four months.

And although her handbag was eventually found in the nearby River Cart, it did not yield any clues. The only item police found, which was to prove significant in time, was a sanitary towel that had been lying near the woman's frozen body curled up in a garage doorway. It suggested that the murder might have been the angry act of a man denied the ultimate sexual favour. Frustrated as they were by the fruitlessness of their investigations, the police were wary of such facile speculation; but the clue took on a new meaning when, some eighteen months later, a group of children playing in a derelict Bridgeton tenement, reported finding the body of what was to be considered ...

Victim No. 2

Like Patricia Docker, 32-year-old Jemima McDonald was a single mother – this time of three children – who liked to go dancing to keep her spirits up. And she didn't have far to go, for the rough-edged glamour and glitter of the Barrowland Ballroom was only about half a mile from her home, one of the few habitable tenements then remaining in the otherwise-derelict area near Bridgeton Cross.

But when she set off for the dance-hall on the evening of Saturday 16 August 1969, wearing a short black skirt, white frilly blouse and high-heeled slingback shoes, it was to be her last visit. She had left her children (aged twelve, nine and seven) in the care of her sister and neighbour, Margaret, who was not particularly concerned about her non-appearance the next day.

Not immediately at least; not until the 'body-in-the-house' reports of the neighbours' playing children, which had been initially shrugged off as a reference to a down-and-out sleeping rough, began to get too persistent and colourful. With mounting anxiety, Margaret waited another day for her sister to appear, then went to investigate the children's story. She was appalled to find Jemima's body lying in the bed-recess of a broken-down tenement flat only a block away. She was partly clothed and had been strangled with her own tights.

It did not take long for the investigating CID officers to draw parallels with the Patricia Docker case. There were so many similarities, it was hard to write them off as coincidences: both women had been to the Barrowland Ballroom; both had been killed in roughly the same way; and both had been menstruating at the time. The last similarity was particularly strange and the police began seriously to consider that they were dealing not only with a double-murderer but also one who might be some sort of sexual deviant.

This time, their dance-hall enquiries were to prove a little more illuminating, thanks to their promise that the 'domestic problems' of potential witnesses would be respected. Thus it came to light that Jemima had been seen leaving the ballroom in the company of an unknown man, and both had been seen walking through the late-night city streets. Within a week a sufficient number of sightings and descriptions of the man had been reported for the police to complete a fairly precise picture of him. It is interesting to note at this point the features that were soon to crop up again. He was described as slim, between twenty-five and thirty-five years old, at least six feet tall, with short reddish-fair hair, wearing a good suit and a white shirt.

Two of the witnesses who helped compile this picture, a boy and a girl, were asked to pin it down even more literally with the help of the American photo-fit system. But when they seemed less than confident about this, an artist was called in – Lennox Paterson, of Glasgow School of Art – who talked to them separately and frequently at some length. From these chats ('to the girl, the wanted man was almost like a film star and definitely a ladies' man') Paterson eventually managed to 'see' the man ... to create an impressionistic-but-firm portrait of him; and for the first time in Scotland, the Crown Office sanctioned the publication of a picture of the suspect in a major crime.

The police were elated. The picture, published in newspapers throughout the country and shown repeatedly on television, was just the tool they needed in their hunt for the killer, and hopes for its success were high. But to their surprise, it made no difference at all and, slowly, the leads dried up again. Not even the offer of £100 reward, scraped together by Jemima's family, could tease out new clues, and those optimistic hopes turned into a sour disappointment which was not relieved by the dance-hall's management calling time on the police presence there. Enough was enough, they said; with the best will in the world, they could help no further; and business, already suffering because of the two murders, stood little chance of recovering while the police were about. Aware that they might need the management's co-operation again in the future, the police decided to preserve goodwill and pull out. It was a decision they were to regret bitterly. For no sooner had they done so than it happened again. Within a matter of days, and within several hundred yards of the safety of her home, the body was found of ...

Victim No. 3
It was only ten weeks after the McDonald murder that attractive 29-year-old Helen Puttock announced to her surprisingly tolerant husband, George – home on leave from a British Army base in Germany – that she was going to the Barrowland for a night out with her sister, Jeannie. Having been sympathetic to the gregarious Helen's social frustration when she had earlier joined him briefly abroad,

George raised no objection to baby-sitting their two children: as he missed them so much while away, he was happy to play the father role whenever he could.

Like Jemima McDonald, Helen was wearing a short black dress as she prepared to leave her temporary home at her mother's in Earl Street, Scotstoun, at about 8.30 p.m. George showed concern for her safe return, handing over some money for a taxi home as she and her sister departed, but he was never to see his wife alive again.

At seven the next morning – Friday 31 October 1969 – roadman Archie MacIntyre was out walking his black labrador when it suddenly made off excitedly towards what looked like a bundle of rags lying in a back-court only a couple of blocks from Helen's home. Responding to the dog's whining, Archie went over to investigate 'and got the shock of my life: it was a woman's body and it was a funny colour ...'

He rushed to a phone-box an dialled 999. And when the police and ambulance services arrived, they confirmed that she was dead. She had been raped and strangled with one of her own stockings; one of her legs was thus bare, there was bruising to her face, and she too had been menstruating: her sanitary towel was found tucked neatly under her arm. But nobody knew who she was ... until, reacting to the flurry of police activity just down the street from where he was living, George Puttock emerged to tell the officers that he was worried about his wife's non-appearance. They showed him the body and his worst fears were confirmed.

Now the manhunt took on an unprecedented intensity. A maniac was clearly at large and had to be stopped before he struck yet again. And the chances of stopping him looked better than ever before – thanks largely to the remarkable recall of Helen's sister. Jeannie Williams had chatted to 'John' not only at the dance-hall but also in a taxi shared with him and Helen part of the way home, and she thus proved to be a superb witness. She was highly valued as such by one of the key senior officers in the hunt, Detective Superintendent Joe Beattie, who personally interviewed her frequently and gleaned detail after detail with great follow-up potential. Such as ...

— The meticulous description of the man who danced with her sister – a description that uncannily matched that of Jemima McDonald's last escort.

— The way his polite manner exploded into authoritative anger at the management when the dance-hall's cigarette machine wouldn't work for Helen.

— How, on the shared taxi ride across the city, he revealed that despite being a non-smoker, he had had cigarettes all the time; he produced a packet of Embassy, grudgingly shared them round, and re-pocketed them without taking one himself.

— His enthusiastic references to golf, including a story about how his cousin had recently scored a hole in one.

— His disdainful attitude to the dance-hall as a 'den of iniquity' frequented by 'adulterous women'.

— His self-righteous statement, when asked in the taxi what he did at New Year, that he preferred praying to drinking. Closely followed by something along the same lines that was to catch and hold the public's imagination for years ...

— His indirect quotation from the Bible, about Moses and a woman who had been stoned, vaguely recognizable from the Old Testament.

In addition to all this, Jeannie was invaluable in helping to enhance the artist's impression of the man who – thanks to the popular touch of a Glasgow news editor – soon became known throughout the land as 'Bible John'. Indeed, Jeannie's own picture of the man was so comprehensive that Superintendent Beattie asserted that he now knew the suspect so well he would recognize him instantly if they passed on the street. It was a meeting that, alas, was never to happen. But not for want of trying ...

Every conceivable angle was taken in the massive exercise to hunt down Bible John. No fewer than one hundred detectives, now openly linking all three murders, were assigned to the case and every police force in the country was asked to cooperate. All the dentists in Glasgow were asked to check their chart records in an attempt to find the overlapping front tooth that might belong to a young man answering John's description; and all the city's tailors were asked to remember such a man ordering high-lapelled suits. Hairdressers' shops were checked out in the hope of finding someone who had done John's unfashionable trim; golf clubs were visited to try to track down his hole-in-one cousin; and because of his military bearing, British and NATO bases all over the world were asked to run through all their leave-pass records. A total of 50,000 statements were taken from nurses and newspapermen, dancers and dance-hall staff, hoteliers and publicans, prison and Borstal officials, ministers and priests, doctors and mental hospital staff, bus drivers and taxi drivers – especially the one who drove the threesome home, though he could unfortunately remember very little about them.

At one point, the world-famous Dutch clairvoyant Gerard Croiset was even called in to help. In response to feelers from the police, the Glasgow-based *Daily Record* brought him to Glasgow in the hope that he could add the Bible John case to his amazing list of psychic successes – which included finding, via the telephone, missing persons as far away from his Utrecht home as America and Japan. In this case the old Einstein-like figure (who has since died) immediately started to draw pictures from his mind of the area where he thought Bible John might be found and, with only the help of a city map, he indicated this to be in the south-west, around Govan. He then focused in on the place, describing old cars near a large defunct engine, schools, recreation grounds, and shops –

one of which he pinpointed, sketching out descriptions of the shopkeepers and an elderly male customer who, he said, was somehow connected to the murderer.

Touring the area, a reporter from the paper found a location similar to this, near a main road, with old cars and a massive, rusting diesel engine. The police quickly responded, checking out the schools and shops and carrying out extensive door-to-door enquiries. Once more, they drew a complete blank … and yet, the lead was tantalizingly close to making sense. One witness interviewed earlier had reported seeing, on a late bus coming from the direction of Helen's home on the night of her murder, a bleeding, breathless and dishevelled young man who alighted near Gray Street, within walking distance of the terminal for the all-night ferry across the Clyde … to Govan.

Could he have been Bible John? If so, that was the last ever sighting of him. He remains doggedly elusive to this day, despite the assiduous efforts not only of the police but also of the media. Indeed, the media was so active in the hunt – there was even an BBC-TV appeal to the culprit couched in biblical terms – that members of the public became in turn enthusiastic detectives. Young men who were unfortunate enough to look like the widely-circulated portrait of Bible John were constantly being challenged in the street. One such man, a printer called Norman MacDonald, was so badgered in this way by passers-by and police-officers that – once eliminated from enquiries – he had to be issued with a special certificate from the Chief Constable to tell would-be apprehenders that he was definitely not Bible John.

But there were real suspects too. One result of a renewed police presence on the Barrowland dance-floor – they were jokingly called the Police Formation Team and teased each other about eyeing up the men rather than the women – was the production of a rather elusive Bible John lookalike who, when finally apprehended and put into an identity parade, obviously did not look quite *enough* like the suspect. Jeannie Williams, who attended over three hundred such parades, failed to identify anybody in this one and the man was promptly released.

The long, frustrating months turned into years with little or no progress to show for the thousands of arduous hours put into the investigation. But the long-standing impact of the case on the public imagination was graphically illustrated in 1977 ... and again as late as 1983 ... when the press came up with 'sensational developments' related to the possible identity of Bible John.

In December 1977, the *Daily Record* splashed a story which claimed that 'a man suspected by many senior policemen to be Bible John has been interviewed about the unsolved murders of four women in Scotland this year' – and the writer, Arnot McWhinnie, went on to say that he had known the identity of the man, an electrician from a town in the west, for as long as seven years 'but I was sworn to secrecy as he had been sent to a mental hospital after admitting the vicious rape of a young woman'. Three years later, McWhinnie published a sensational interview with the man in which he denied being Bible John although he 'understood' why police suspected him, and added: 'I have an innocent explanation for everything.' One such thing was the fact that he had been to a dentist to have his two front teeth removed; he claimed this was because of a football injury.

And in February 1983, there was a renewed flurry of interest in the Bible John story, when a heating engineer called Harry Wylie suddenly went public with his private suspicions about his one-time best friend, David Henderson, who had gone to live in Holland in 1970. In their younger days, in the late sixties, they had often gone to the Barrowland Ballroom together – though they had not always left together – and Harry had long found David to be 'the double of the Bible John drawing'. So obsessed did Wylie become with this thought that he even hired private detectives to check out Henderson, 'hoping they would prove me wrong; but as their investigation went on, the more coincidences kept cropping up'.

The accusation drew big headlines, but after Henderson had made a spirited defence of himself, also through newspaper columns – 'What's Harry trying to do to me? The whole thing is a load of rubbish' – the episode ended in a farcical catalogue of embarrassment and recrimination. And for the police, who had kept a restrained objectivity throughout, it was once again back to square one ...

One of the strangest aspects of the very strange Bible John story is the sudden appearance, and equally sudden ending, of his deadly works. If his urge to kill was so overwhelming that he had to yield to it three times, why did he suddenly stop? Or did he? There have since been similar murders in other parts of Scotland – and England, and even further afield – that remain unsolved. Did he simply move down south? Did proven guilt of some less serious offence see his removal to a mental institution?

There could be other explanations. Did he simply die – naturally, accidentally, or even by his own hand driven by remorse? It is also possible that Bible John could have 'grown out' of his psychopathic tendencies and may now be living a normal life, no longer driven by the compulsion to kill. To quote a leading psychiatrist: 'He will still be fully aware of what he has done in the past and will be carrying with him the terrible guilt and shame of it. But his conscience will not be strong enough to make him confess, although he will no longer have the urge to kill again.'

There is, of course, another theory which would demand a radical rethink of many assumptions. As one high-level Scots law officer puts it quite bluntly: 'There was no such person as Bible John.' He believes that the three murders could have been the work of two, or even three, different people. And, of course, it is not unknown for follow-up crimes in a series to be committed by a copy-cat to throw all the blame on to the first culprit. Could the two later murders have been the work of two copy-cat killers?

There are so many possibilities, but the consensus of experienced opinion still tends to come down on the one-killer theory. And what is certain is that, despite all the high-quality description and evidence that police have had to hand, the killer of each of these women was clever enough to elude one of the biggest dragnets ever cast in any manhunt anywhere. And there is now very little hope of finding him unless something – something he reads in the Bible perhaps? – prompts him to come forward and come clean. But until that happens, *his conscience will not be strong enough to make him confess* ...

10   The Unknown Bairn, 1971

Though it was a spring afternoon, the cold rain was spitting into their faces and the dark sky cast a miserable gloom over what was to have been a happy little outing for the father and his five-year-old son. They were walking slowly along the shingle beach, kicking a few pebbles before them, wondering what to do next, when the father saw it first. A multi-coloured floating object being washed back and forth perhaps two or three yards out in the grey waves lapping on to the southern bank of the Tay estuary. 'I thought it was a plastic doll.' As he was wearing his wellingtons, he scrunched over the seaweed at the water's edge, waded in, grasped the object, and turned it over ...

For Ian Robertson, a postman in the little Fife town of Tayport, the afternoon of Sunday 23 May 1971, started off as a disappointment and turned into a black memory that he knows will never leave him. At the pretty boating pond on the town's east-end common hard by the fast-flowing river, the weather had been playing havoc with what had been a much-anticipated event ... the first model-boat race there since the beginning of the war. It would have been just the thing to amuse his little boy, Neil, but when they realized it was going to be a literal wash-out, they turned away and headed across the shore-track for that teeth-gritting walk along the rough little nearby beach.

It wasn't to be a long walk. Less than a hundred yards from the pond, near a large jagged chunk of rock sticking up through the pebbles like a sore thumb, the discovery of the floating thing stopped them in their tracks. Puzzled,

Neil waited obediently on the beach as he watched the bundle being turned over; then, strangely, his father suddenly shouted to him – to go home at once. He wanted to ask 'Why?' but the stridency in his dad's voice told him it was no-questions-asked order. He turned and ran home.

Later, when he was older and could understand, his father answered his unasked question. 'When I turned the bundle over, it was a quite horrible sight – to see that it was a human body. A little boy about three years old. The nose and lips were almost gone and the knees were in a bad shape, all points where the body would have been in friction with the rocks or the river-bed.'

With Neil safely out of range, Ian, trembling with shock and cold, brought the body on to the beach and ran back to the common, where the model-boatmen were packing up. 'I had to get one of them back to confirm what I had seen, it seemed so much like a bad dream.' And indeed, his volunteer saw the same ghastly sight and reacted with similar shocked disbelief. At once, they called in the police and soon the little body, wearing a patterned pyjama-type jersey over a blue shirt, was off to the pathologist in Cupar – who later concluded that the boy had met his death by drowning.

But if the submission of his remains to the machinery of authority prompted hope that grieving parents would now materialize to round off the tragic matter with some dignity, to give the boy at least a loving burial, that hope was a vain one.

For incredible as it may seem, to this day no one – not a parent or grandparent, not even a distant relative – has come forward to identify or claim him. And it could not be for lack of publicity: there was almost daily coverage of the story in the Scottish press at the time; or for lack of police effort, which stretched from the banks of the Tay to Interpol involvement in the coastal countries of mainland Europe. He must have come from somewhere; he must have been missed by someone. The alternative seems almost unthinkable: that he was unwanted, forcibly drowned, and allowed to slip away with the tide. But why? Such a fate is more commonly reserved for unwanted new-born babies. How many parents, however evil or distressed, could commit such a deed against a little one with whom they had lived for a few years? Or had he died with his parents, either accidentally or in a suicide pact? That might explain, to some degree, the lack of response. But where then did the adult bodies go? None was ever found that could be connected to the boy.

Every year, on the anniversary of the sad discovery, local people still gather at the west-side cemetery in a belated effort to make up for the love that somehow, somewhere, the little boy lost along the way. But the grim fact that not all people are so compassionate and caring is also acknowledged here. For among those who come to lay down their floral tributes and say their silent prayers will often be a plain-clothes policeman. On the assumption that a killer could be remorseful enough to visit his victim's resting place, each face is checked that gazes down on the simple three-foot stone. And somehow, despite such visits, the little boy seems still alone, even at rest, for there is a certain sad irony in the positioning of the grave – by itself, some distance away from the rows of community graves on the bank of the river directly facing the cityscape of Dundee; the very river that may have claimed his life. Engraved on the plain-faced granite, free of charge by local stone sculptor Robert Lawson, are the words:

Erected by the people of Scotland
In memory of
THE UNKNOWN BAIRN
A wee boy
Aged between 2 and 4 years
Found on the beach at Tayport
23rd May 1971
'Suffer little children to come unto me'

The stone was not yet in place when the boy was put to rest five days after he was found. In contrast to that miserable afternoon, however, it was a fine sunny day that blossomed for the simple, if very well attended, burial ceremony. Local undertaker John Beat remembers how, in the absence of relatives, he carefully handed over the small white-covered coffin he had made to the gravedigger 'who then descended some specially-dug steps to place it gently in the grave'. The minister's accompanying words touched the hearts of the sizeable crowd that had gathered and there was many a silent tear, even from the hardened men of the police and the press, and certainly from those who had seen to it that at least the little lad was receiving a respectful farewell.

One such person was the then-provost of the village, James Pow, who himself said a few poignant words to the press that still reflect the emotions of the townsfolk: 'My wife and I are heartbroken over this.' And his own emotion clearly lives on today as he recalls his part in bringing the case to public attention:

> When I heard about the finding of the body, I feared the arrangements for his burial were going to be pretty rough, so I organised a fund-raising campaign with the help of the press, to give him a proper funeral and gravestone. It was amazing. The money just flooded in from all over Scotland and beyond and the townhouse staff couldn't do any other work for a couple of weeks. We ended up with far too much, so the remainder went to the SSPCC.

And so, almost two decades later, the mystery of the Unknown Bairn remains unsolved and continues to haunt and trouble the people of Tayport who were involved in the strange and perplexing affair. And even those who were not ...

The story of the Unknown Bairn had clearly saddened, moved and mystified the whole country. Considering the coverage it received, it was impossible to imagine that, even south of the border, the case had not been heard of. 'So the questions everybody was asking were: did the boy fall in the water or was he put in? If he was put in ... why? And if he fell in, why did the parents not come forward? And even if the parents had drowned too, where was the rest of his family?' There is still an ache in Mr Pow's voice as he expresses the desperate hope that some day, somehow, the truth will be known.

But the police and the press, the two forces that could extract that truth if anyone could, were repeatedly frustrated at the time, and their efforts then were so tireless and thorough – the police pushing hard on many investigative fronts, the press diligently reporting progress and inviting feedback – that it now seems hopelessly optimistic to expect some lucky breakthrough in the future. There was perhaps a little justification for optimism in the early period of the investigation but, as the diary of police progress gleaned from daily reports shows, this slowly but surely soured into chronic frustration ...

– 23 May: Body is found; police alerted. The only clue they find is the maker's label on one of his items of clothing: 'Achilles, size 3'. They say the child, found on the foreshore at high-water mark beside the saw-mill at Tayport, is aged 'about two to three' and is almost three feet tall.

— 24 May: Post-mortem reveals that the boy's death was due to drowning and that he had been in the water for two to six weeks.

— 25 May: Growing puzzlement over lack of family response to press reports. Detective-Superintendent James Morgan, of Fife Constabulary, says: 'We agree there are suspicious circumstances. No child has been reported missing to our knowledge.' Appeals to police forces along the east coast and banks of the Tay, other UK forces, and the Missing Persons Bureau in London, have all proved negative.

— 26 May: Inquiries extended to continental countries, British and foreign ships checked; so far in vain. The label clue has revealed that the shirt was made by a Leeds firm, John Barren & Co, which distributed all over the UK and discontinued the line some five years before. Suggests boy came from less-than-wealthy family clothing its children with hand-me-downs or second-hand items. Also suggests that he was British.

— 27 May: First possible breakthrough. Police say it has been established that a pair of child's 'Rainger' wellingtons were found near the spot of boy's discovery thirteen days before. Inside one leg, the name 'K. Gerrard' had been written with felt-tipped pen; the boots contained a pair of fawn ankle socks, and a clean white handkerchief was lying nearby. 'It is thought these may have been left by a child prior to paddling in the water.'

— 28 May: Burial ceremony, 'Provost appeals for gravestone for unknown child' – headline in *Dundee Courier*. 'I hope this appeal is not long under way before relatives of the poor wee bairn turn up to claim him,' comments Mr Pow in the report below. 'Often families split up but usually there is a grandmother or somebody …' Frustration is clearly mounting.

— 29 May: Money starts to pour in, but no progress so far on 'wellington' lead.

— 31 May: Another promising tip-off. A couple of travelling people have been overheard talking on a bus, from Leven to Dunfermline, about a lost boy. 'I lost my wee boy that day and he was only two,' the woman is reported to have told her long-dark-haired male companion. She is described as aged forty to fifty, short, with ruddy complexion.

— 1 June: Massive response to provost's gravestone appeal. Letters, poems, donations pouring in to the town clerk's office, including gifts of 75p from a group of five

Dundee children and 25p from 'Sharon, who cares'. Local girl footballers donate all the takings from their match.

— 2 June: The travelling folk lead crumbles. Police have tracked down the couple to find that the woman was talking about the day her son was taken into care. But they say 'intensive inquiries' are still going on among travelling communities.

— 5 June: Chief Superintendent White, head of Fife CID, expresses 'amazement' at lack of response from the boy's family and reveals that the 'wellington' clue has been eliminated. He stresses that the victim was not necessarily a 'travelling' boy. But ...

— 9 June: A general alert goes out to trace a 'tinker' woman who was selling lavender in the area 'about three weeks ago'. Leads are obviously becoming thinner and weaker.

— 10 June: As local, national and international police inquiries yield nothing, what is perhaps the final hope has to be abandoned. Suggestions that there might have been a connection with a body washed up at Kingsbarns two nights before, on the other side of the Fife peninsula, are discounted after it is revealed that the body – of an elderly woman with no teeth and wearing only the remains of a woollen vest and a corset – had been in the water for several months. 'It is thus considered unlikely,' says Detective-Superintendent Morgan, 'that there is any link with the child found at Tayport.'

With a depressing certainty, the leads dried up and left the police scratching around for clues. Though they kept the case file open, there was nowhere left for them to turn. It seemed, and seems still, quite unbelievable that a little boy who once had a name, a family, a home, a language and a culture could, in death, no longer have anything to which he might be connected.

For the many perplexed people who cared, all that

remained to assuage the frustration of not understanding was simple speculation. Yet most of their theories crumble under close examination.

A coastguard at Fife Ness, for example, suggested that the boy might have been washed all the way over from a continental country and (assuming that Interpol had been less intensive in its inquiries than the UK police) his relatives might not have considered the possibility of his ending up on the other side of the North Sea. 'I certainly wouldn't rule that out,' he said. 'Given the right conditions of wind and tide, the body could have come right across.'

But the British label on his clothes clearly suggested that he was, if not Scottish, English. And indeed, the coastguard had to concede that the 'more probable' explanation was that the body had been washed down-river. 'There are about three strong tidal streams around the Tay estuary,' he said, 'and they make such a complicated network that an object's movements would be almost impossible to trace back through them. It's a vicious river with very strong currents.'

Another popular theory – actually put forward in the early days of the investigation by Detective-Superintendent Morgan himself – was that the boy had been on board a ship at sea with his family; there had been an incident and all had drowned. But there were no subsequent reports of lost or abandoned vessels and no other bodies recovered.

Now retired and with plenty of time to reflect on one of the most challenging cases of his career, Mr Morgan today rejects 'ship' theories and 'foreign' theories – 'We've never had anyone come right across the North Sea' – and finds himself, after all those years, resorting inevitably to his still-strong policeman's instinct.

I can't really say why, but I always felt, and feel even more strongly these days, that the boy was reasonably local and the child of poor parents who were perhaps too short of money to give him decent burial after accidental drowning and/or too embarrassed to come forward and try to do so while all the publicity was going on.

Why from a poor family?

Well, all we really had to go on were his clothes and, while exposure to the water had certainly added to their wear and tear quite considerably, they were not of good quality in the first place and were also probably hand-me-downs.

By poor, does he perhaps mean travelling-folk?

Not necessarily. He could have been from a poor family across the river in Dundee – we had cases like that before, of bodies just floating over to the Fife side – but, yes, my feeling is that he was a child of the travelling folk and had come down river from, say, Perthshire. They are, let's face it, a little lax about the bureaucracy that the rest of us have grudgingly learned to live with; they don't follow the press as avidly as most people, they don't follow the rules, and it's not unknown for them to leave a death unregistered. But they are good people with their children, very fond and loving with them, and would probably be very sad about not being able to give a youngster like this a proper funeral.

Perhaps they did, in their own way. Perhaps they sang their songs for him and prayed for him around a campfire. For some people of nature, unable and perhaps even unwilling to fund a 'proper' funeral, such an exit might even be desirable; the most natural burial of all. And for those of a more urban culture who still care and wonder, such a thought could be a consoling one …

For, despite all the evidence to the contrary, the Unknown Bairn must still be known to someone … affectionately remembered, let's hope, by those who were closest to him; who nurtured him, played with him, fed him, and loved him.

It may not be too much to hope. As Mr Morgan says, 'somebody always puts fresh flowers on his grave'.

11   Pilot Error?, 1975

To drive around the magnificence of Mull, looking up in awe as you weave through haughty sheep contemptuous of your approach, is to realize just how small you are. Empty and looming, the island emphatically reminds you that it still belongs to God; that the tracks Man has made here for his little machines are but pathetic and barely-tolerated scratches on its face. One of these scratches was put there in 1965, on the east shore of the Sound of Mull ten miles south of Tobermory, by men of the Royal Engineers. It is a half-mile-long grassy landing-strip attached to the wooden Norwegian-log Glenforsa Hotel and much used by its more prosperous guests with access to private aircraft.

One such guest, staying for a few days around Christmas 1975, was property manager Peter Gibbs. By all accounts, this former Spitfire pilot was an exceptional man – darkly handsome, much younger looking than his fifty-four years, separated from his wife, and still something of a flying adventurer. 'In flying he took things to the limit,' his son Michael said of him. 'He enjoyed doing exciting things: he liked – not dicing with death but dicing on the edge of life.' And not only did he have a distinguished flying career behind him, but he could also boast high-flying achievement in the world of music, having been leader of the BBC Scottish Symphony Orchestra.

Although latterly based in Highbury, London, that harmonious experience had made him fond of Scotland,

and particularly of Mull, which he knew well after many previous visits. Indeed, so enthusiastic was he about the island that he was contemplating the purchase of a hotel there, a subject that must have figured large in his conversations with his attractive 33-year-old friend, Dr Felicity Grainger, who accompanied him on the Christmas visit. They had arrived by car – Gibbs' elderly Jaguar – but there was no way such a man could ensconce himself in a hotel so temptingly near to an active landing-strip without feeling the overpowering desire to fly. Thus, when he heard that a single-engined Cessna 150 was available for hire across the water at Oban's North Connel airport, he soon had the machine back at Glenforsa with his hands on its controls.

Gibbs hired the plane from Ian Hamilton, a former Scottish sheriff with a colourful past who, as a student, had been involved in the controversial removal of the Stone of Scone from Westminster Abbey on Christmas Day 1955. He was not to know that his arrangement with Gibbs would involve him in big headlines again, exactly twenty years later. Nor did he know, as he handed over the £3,000 plane he had bought the previous September (to service a market-garden business) that a month after that Peter Gibbs' flying-licence had lapsed. When Gibbs explained that he had come on holiday without his licence because he had not expected to fly, Hamilton gave him the benefit of the doubt – also because his own telephonic inquiries, and the obvious expertise demonstrated by Gibbs in pre-flight checks, convinced him that here was an accomplished pilot.

It is probably fair to say that Gibbs' expertise then was as impressive as it had ever been; but his licence had not been renewed for other reasons. He was not as young as he looked, and, on applying for his renewal after a medical examination the previous May, he had been told to undergo a general flying test (which he had not yet done) and it was written into his record that he should wear spectacles to correct near/distance vision when flying. In the light of this problem, however slight he might have perceived it to be, the strange decision he took at around 9 p.m. on Christmas Eve seemed all the more incomprehensible. It was a fatal decision that was to create not one disturbing mystery but three, the one materializing on the heels of the other as each was solved. And to this day, the third has never been adequately explained ...

Less of a mystery, more a puzzle, was why in the first place such an experienced pilot should choose to don his flying-gear at that time of night on Christmas Eve, a few hours before his fifty-fifth birthday, and walk out of the hotel with the stated intention of taking off into the darkness. Felicity Grainger, who accompanied him, later claimed that he had been anxious to test himself and the airstrip for night landing, being of the opinion that its night closure inhibited its usefulness as the only strip on the island. 'It was just something that he wanted to know. It was not a sudden impulse.'

Yet it did not take any kind of a pilot to realize that an attempt even by someone with perfect eyesight to try to land on an unlit strip like this would be fraught with danger. Indeed, though he 'did not know much about airplanes', the manager of the hotel, Tim Howitt, advised Gibbs that such a flight was not wise and tried to discourage him.

'He said he was not asking my permission,' the hotelier recalled later, 'but letting me know his intentions as a courtesy and did not want any fuss.' Thus shrugging off the warning, Gibbs disappeared into the night with Grainger and soon the Cessna's Rolls Royce Continental engine burst into life. It attracted something of an audience: disbelieving guests gathered to watch its taxi-ing lights from the observation lounge that looked out across the Sound of Mull to the mainland, as Tim Howitt's brother David and his wife Pauline rushed out from their nearby chalet to look, astonished, through their binoculars. From different vantages, both Tim and Pauline Hewitt saw strange lights around the plane's wings before it took off. These were subsequently assumed to have come from the two hand-torches Grainger said she took with her to help guide Gibbs in. But the lights were alleged – by both onlookers – to have been too far apart to come from torches held by one person. And as Grainger later told an inquiry that Gibbs had not got out of the plane to assist her, this was another puzzling factor – was there anyone else out there? 'I assumed,' said Tim Howitt, 'that there were two other people with torches.' In the absence of any further evidence, however, there was no development of this intriguing point. Yet it was a puzzle that could hardly compare in magnitude to …

Mystery No. 1

Whatever happened to the plane and pilot?

By the time the Cessna had revved up and taken off, David Howitt had walked down to within a few yards of the runway in time to gasp at its silhouetted shape roaring past his head at about a hundred feet – with its landing lights going off, on and off again. He could still see it as it climbed to about 800 feet out across the Sound in the direction of the mainland. When it turned on to an easterly heading, both he and the other observers assumed it was executing a normal circuit which involved turning back across the Sound and slipping briefly out of sight behind some high coastal pine trees, before descending to approach the runway from the east. 'This usually means an aircraft will re-appear from behind the trees within about 15 seconds,' says David Howitt, a journalist with some flying experience himself, who also supervises the hotel airstrip. 'But this plane did not re-appear and, after a while, assuming Gibbs had another flight-plan in mind, my wife and I made our way back to our chalet. That was when, turning back briefly, I saw the light on the water of the Sound.'

The light? 'Both my wife and I assumed it was a flare, which lasted perhaps 20 seconds before fading and disappearing. I then thought it possible that the plane might have undershot the runway and crashed into the

Sound.' But he was less than convinced and preferred to believe that the light had come from a passing trawler … that the plane's pilot, wisely deciding that a night landing here looked too hazardous, had climbed well above the surrounding 3,000-ft mountains and contacted Glasgow or Prestwick for a safer course to either of these airports with night-landing facilities. And as such route-request communications could be intercepted by radio, Howitt hurried into his chalet, picked up his special set which could be tuned into aircraft transmissions, and scanned from 108 to 136 Mhz, hoping to pick up a distress call from the Cessna. But in vain. With a growing sense of unease, he then drove half a mile along the shore road, as near as possible to the point where he had seen the 'flare' on the water, and scanned the whole area with his car's headlights. Also without success. His unease began to border on alarm as, just before 10 p.m., sleet started to fall and he realized Gibbs then had no chance of returning to Glenforsa that night.

On return to his father's hotel, he found a shivering Felicity Grainger being comforted by some guests. Paradoxically, while their anxiety was increasing – soon the plane would have little fuel left and the weather had rapidly deteriorated – she would hear nothing pessimistic. She seemed sure that Gibbs ('not a man to take risks') knew what he was doing and, explaining that she did not want to spoil everyone's Christmas Eve by being unduly alarmist, asked that no telephone check-calls or alerting calls to the police be made until 10.30, by which time the plane could have landed somewhere else.

But the calls made immediately after 10.30 established that it had not; and within half an hour, the first two-man volunteer search party was moving out of the Glenforsa Hotel, soon to become the frenetically busy HQ of a major search-and-rescue operation. But although this grew over the next two weeks into probably the biggest such hunt ever mobilized in Scotland, with police and mountain rescue teams and RAF planes covering a 150-mile radius, it proved frustratingly fruitless. Not the tiniest clue to the whereabouts of the plane and/or its pilot was uncovered.

It was as if they had vanished into thin air. And in the absence of rational explanations, the Great Mull Air Mystery began to take on irrational, even supernatural ones. The Press was full of romantic theorizing, the island hummed with wide-eyed gossip and invention. A local driver on the mainland swore he had seen the plane crash into the Sound – several weeks before it actually disappeared. The hotel's room 14, in which Gibbs and Grainger had slept, became a room-with-a-presence to be avoided because two other people who had stayed there also died in aircraft accidents: Prince William of Gloucester and Glasgow flying instructor Lesley Butler. Even the Howitt brothers' mother succumbed. She insisted she had seen a young man answering Gibbs' description walking across the Glenforsa runway in full wartime RAF flying-gear shortly after his disappearance.

But in reality, her son David had, unknowingly, come nearest to the truth. As one half of that first urgently-arranged search party on Christmas Eve – the other was local police constable Alec MacLennan – he had trekked, through increasingly hostile weather, up hundreds of feet of spongy, slipper hillside (over which the plane would have descended on its final approach about a mile south of the runway) in the reasonable hope that if the crash had happened here, the pilot might still be alive. The two men separated and searched intensely through the trees and driving sleet with powerful torches. They were looking for something obvious, like flames or a broken wing protruding from the undergrowth. But Howitt later realized that, if he had known he was looking only for a man, things might have turned out quite differently ...

For nearly four months later, when both men returned to the area on a spring-bright April morning – summoned to help officials identify a body found by shepherd Donald MacKinnon – he realised that he could not have been more than a hundred yards away from that spot as he searched the hillside that fateful night. The body was lying backwards over the fallen trunk of a larch, 400 feet up the hill from the now-serene water of the Sound of Mull, and exactly a mile from the near-end of Glenforsa runway.

'Yes,' said Howitt, as he gazed on the once-handsome features now grotesquely disfigured by weather and crows, 'I am certain that is Peter Gibbs.' Dental records later confirmed this. And Gibbs' clothes, though now faded, were as Howitt remembered them – lightweight cord slacks, checked shirt, pale blue pullover, and flying-boots. But the stench of decay was something he would rather forget, and he was glad to turn back down the hill with the vaguely satisfying feeling that at least part of the mystery had been solved.

But he hadn't reached the road at the foot of the hill before more questions began to raise themselves. If Gibbs' body had been there for four months, on a spot regularly passed by a shepherd with his dogs, why had it not been found before now? The body's legs had been straddled around one of the larch's upgrowing branches, as if trapping it in a fall – why would Gibbs have been coming *down* the mountain? And, perhaps most pertinent of all, the question that was to remain tantalizingly unanswered for more than a decade …

Mystery No. 2
Where then was the plane?

If the position of Gibbs' body suggested that he had been coming downhill, the logical conclusion to reach was that he had crashed and abandoned the plane at a higher altitude, not far from where he was found. Indeed, Chief Inspector Malcolm MacMartin, in charge of the inquiry, said as much: 'The reasonable assumption now is that Mr Gibbs crashed the plane somewhere up the hill, had a miraculous escape from death or injury, walked down the hill, and succumbed to exposure.'

But as the machine was nowhere to be found on nearby land, it was assumed – briefly – that it must have plunged into one of two small fresh-water lochs within a few miles of the body's final position. This theory did not hold up, however, on two major counts – the virtual impossibility of a shocked Gibbs covering so much difficult terrain to get to where he was found, and the shallowness of the lochs: a quick survey revealed that there was no evidence in either of them of leaked oil, floating debris, or protruding parts.

So perhaps, realizing he was in trouble, Gibbs had simply jumped out of the plane and allowed it to fly on by itself to crash into the Sound below? Felicity Grainger claimed this is what Gibbs had always said he would do in an emergency; but the absence of serious injury to his body – there was only a three-inch cut on the left shin – established beyond reasonable doubt that this was not what had happened. And at the fatal accident inquiry held in Oban on 24 June 1976, the Board of Trade Accident Inspector William Cairns maintained that it would have been 'extremely difficult' for the pilot to open the plane's door in flight.

With these theories thus more or less dismissed, and the plane still missing, the only remaining possibility seemed to be that Gibbs had indeed undershot the runway over the Sound, come down in the water, and escaped from the Cessna as it sank. This also became a highly unlikely explanation, however, after forensic tests revealed a complete lack of salt-water traces on his clothes, watch, and flying-boots.

But it did not lose all credence, as an element of possibility was raised when David Howitt published a book entitled *The Great Mull Air Mystery* – which suggested that the plane might have come down at a point, just short of the airstrip, where the River Forsa floods into the Sound and puts down a wide layer of *fresh* water on its surface.

For some time, this appeared to be a reasonable supposition in the absence of any others, but it was eventually dramatically invalidated: one of the few questions to be answered by the long-awaited development that had always promised to solve everything, as implied by Procurator Fiscal Graeme Pagan's statement in his inquiry summing-up that 'some mystery will always remain unless the plane can be found ...'

The first tantalizing clue to suggest that the plane had indeed crashed into the Sound appeared nearly four months after that inquiry – when farmer Robert Duncan found an aircraft tyre and inner tube on the shore at Kentallen, several miles north of Glenforsa. After it was established that that the tyre would in fact match the Cessna, and that its covering of marine growth showed that it had been under water for a considerable time, attention was refocused on the Sound.

A subsequent sea search with sonar equipment revealed nothing, however, and the mystery began to grow again – although the evidence that the plane had undershot the runway and sunk remained compelling. Indeed, the little red-and-white Cessna was not to be found until every fantastic theory about its fate had been expounded by expert and layman alike ... until, in fact, almost ten years later. And when it materialized in September 1986, its position was so far from the river-entrance that no further credence could be given to the idea that Gibbs might have swum through a top layer of fresh water to the shore, thus accounting for the lack of salt traces in his clothing.

The plane's finder was professional diver George Foster who, searching for scallops which tend to congregate in shadowy areas, went down to check out what had appeared as a 'promising lump' on his echo sounder. Discerning a dark shape 100 feet down, 500 yards from the shore (and a mile and a half from the runway), he swam straight for it 'and saw to my surprise that it was the body of a plane'. The wings had been parted from it and he saw one lying flat in the mud about 100 yards away. The engine had also separated from the fuselage and one propeller blade was bent back as if it had suffered some impact. 'I didn't fully appreciate the significance of my discovery at the time,' said Foster, 'until I mentioned it to some mates on my return home; they got pretty excited and said I shouldn't tell anyone else for a while.'

But despite not appreciating its importance, Foster was curious enough to examine the wreck and remembers how, on peering inside the cockpit, he felt 'oddly disappointed that there wasn't a body there or something'. He also noticed that the windscreen was 'completely out' and tried to enter the cockpit through it – 'but I just couldn't get in that way with all my gear on'. Still keen to see inside, though, he turned to the doors and tried to open them – 'that was a devil of a job'. When he finally succeeded, all he found inside the cockpit was 'a large, sinister lobster'.

He also noted the absence of compass and radio – and the presence of a single frogman's flipper in the mud, not far from the wreck. So had he in fact been the first to find the plane? He could not be sure.

But what Foster's find had clearly established were two quite vital facts: one, that the doors of the plane had been firmly shut on impact and sinking; and two, that – despite the lack of salt traces on his clothes – Gibbs must have therefore scrambled out of the cockpit through the smashed windscreen. And those being the circumstances, minds would now have to be concentrated on yet another perplexing question in this constantly intriguing case …

Mystery No. 3
Why was the body on the hillside?

Accepting this scenario, it is not hard to imagine the desperate plight of Peter Gibbs in the Cessna's last airborne moments. Realizing that he was undershooting into the Sound, he would have employed all his vast flying experience to retrieve the situation and, failing, would have been shocked and charged with adrenalin – fighting to save himself as the machine smashed into the water. He would have struggled out through the windscreen as it parted company with the wings, thrust himself up and away, then swum for the shore as if his life depended on it – which it did. And this for 25 minutes over a distance of some 500 yards, through bone-chilling water and driving sleet: appalling conditions that would have tested younger and stronger swimmers to the limit.

Yet, having survived to reach the shore, why would he then have crossed two nearby, parallel roads – roads that would have led him straight back to the hotel's warmth and comfort in a few minutes – and opted to struggle on up the hillside for another 400 feet? Even further perhaps, considering the 'downhill' position of his body when found.

It seems nothing short of incredible: that a chill-shocked, soaking and exhausted middle-aged man who had just miraculously escaped death should, for any reason whatsoever, eschew the prospect of salvation and comfort within walking distance and choose instead to climb away from them into the hostile terrain of an incline that can be about 45 degrees in some places. It is a climb that calls for considerable exertion in the best of conditions, and on that night it must have been a nightmare of slithery banks, muddy pitfalls, and spiky trees and bushes. Not to mention two newly-erected barbed-wire fences.

Medical experts have suggested that Gibbs might have been affected by a euphoric disorientation that can be brought on by concussion and would not therefore have been aware of climbing the hillside. But, unlikely though it might seem, he could also have had more rational reasons for making himself scarce after the accident.

Island gossip had it that a surfeit of alcohol could have accounted for what looked like an impulsive decision to take off that fateful Christmas Eve. Toxicology tests on his body had revealed a ratio of about 100mg of alcohol per 100ml of blood (the legal limit is 80) but conclusions were complicated by the presence of organisms, suggesting that this level was 'likely' to have been produced after death.

But while Gibbs was thus officially considered not to have been intoxicated, it is known that at least a little wine had been drunk in his room before his fateful flight. Aware perhaps that even the smallest amount of alcohol in his blood – detected immediately after such a traumatic accident – would complicate his already compromised legality in flying without a licence, he might have simply chosen to sit it out for a while, assessing his plight before returning to the hotel.

Another popular theory was that he might have actually planned to disappear, to 'do a Stonehouse' by parachuting from the plane, and that the plan had been thwarted by the severity of conditions encountered on the ground. Not far above the point where his body was discovered, two walkers came across what they swore was a parachute harness tucked under a rock; but the police, maintaining that it was merely from a rucksack, put it into storage.

Such a scenario would certainly explain the lack of salt traces on his clothing. But there are other ideas on this. One is that the plane could have crashed into shallow water near the shore – with Gibbs clambering out over the dry fuselage – and then drifted out to the position in which it was finally found. Another, which would explain the non-discovery of the body for such a long period, is that he was actually put on the hill some time after his death ... although, in finding that death was due to exposure, the medical officer at the accident inquiry, Dr W.D.S. McLay, said that the body's condition 'was entirely consistent with lying out there for a period of four months'.

(An intriguing aside to this idea was provided by a fiction story anonymously submitted for consideration to Fiona Langford, editor of *Am Muileach*, the island's local paper. She felt it was too close to the real, controversial run of events to publish, but in essence, it suggested that a small plane from Glenforsa had a mysterious assignment to drop flotation bags, with waterproof lights, for picking up by a local trawler. It came down too low, crashed into the water, and its rescued pilot later died on board the boat. His body was such an embarrassment to the trawler crew that they later placed it on a nearby hill.)

Finally: was it just conceivable that salt traces could simply have been washed away if the body had indeed lain out at the mercy of the elements for four months? In an attempt to answer this question, David Howitt arranged for a set of clothes similar to those worn by Gibbs to be dragged for 25 minutes and 500 yards through the water of the Sound. His intention was to leave these exposed to the winter weather for four months and then have them examined for salt traces.

At the time of writing, this exercise had not been completed. Yet were it to prove conclusively that Peter Gibbs could have swum back to the shore through salt water and shown no later sign of having done so, such a finding would be no more than interesting. It would be unlikely to lay all the other questions to rest, with their answers so clearly determined to remain elusive. Indeed, in the perverse way of this long-running and bewildering saga, it would represent more illumination which in turn would serve only to create more mystery.

For it now seems hopelessly optimistic to expect that anyone will ever really know exactly what happened to Peter Gibbs, the flying adventurer, on his last great adventure.

12   Where are They Now?, 1976

This was not, as Chief Constable Donald Henderson explained at Inverness a couple of months after it came to light, a missing-person case in the simple and understood sense of the phrase. 'It is a most peculiar mystery,' he said, 'and despite all the hard work that has been done, all we know is something a little more detailed about the lady's movements on the last day and a lot more about her relationships and her difficulties and things that might have caused it. But as to what happened, and how it happened, we have not got a clue.'

What the senior Inverness officer was referring to in January 1977, was the bizarre disappearance on 12 November the previous year of attractive local housewife Mrs Renee MacRae, and her three-year-old son Andrew. It is a case which has continued to baffle police to this day; and about which the top detective in the investigation, now-retired Superintendent Donald Macarther, said a decade later: 'Never a day passes but I think of Mrs MacRae and particularly the wee boy.' With its piquant element of the missing pair's still-unresolved fate, the enigma has puzzled the people of Scotland probably more than any other comparable case in recent years. One measure of the continuing public fascination with this unfinished story is that, whenever the compilation of this book of mysteries has been mentioned to anyone, the inevitable response has been: 'Oh! It will include the Mrs MacRae mystery of course!'

So how did it all begin, this tragic and bewildering tale?

At about ten o'clock on the Friday night in which Mrs MacRae and her son were later presumed to have disappeared, Malcolm Vaughan, a bus driver from Boat of Garten, was passing a lay-by at Dalmagarry, where the A9 cuts through desolate and misty moorland about twelve miles south of Inverness, when he noticed flames rising from behind the obscuring embankment. He stopped, looked again, and without further hesitation, went forward to investigate. Braving the fierce inferno, he found at the centre of it a metallic blue BMW 1602 turning rapidly into a skeleton as it was eagerly consumed by the flames. After checking that there was no one inside it, he stopped a passing motorist and asked him to call the fire brigade. But by the time it got there, there was little or nothing of the BMW's bodywork and interior left to save. Because of this near-total destruction, detectives were never able to check the car for fingerprints, although it did yield one small, possibly vital, clue …

But one of the first puzzling aspects of the affair was: why did the police take so long to get their investigation under way? They had immediately traced the ownership of the locked car, but without establishing Mrs MacRae's intended whereabouts or seeking to contact her, they left it until the following Monday to probe seriously the circumstances of the blaze and the mysterious vanishing of the mother and son from the scene.

The delay might have been partly because the car was found to be unoccupied and partly because no one had reported Mrs MacRae missing over the weekend. Her estranged husband, Gordon, had no reason to believe that anything was amiss, as she had told him she would be spending the weekend with her sister in Kilmarnock. In fact, it seemed she had other plans for those days, and her husband – with whom she had remained on good terms, despite their break-up – only learned of them later from her closest female friend who, after seeing the wreckage of the car on the Sunday, waited with mounting fear for Mrs MacRae's return. It was when his wife failed to contact him or pick up their nine-year-old son Gordon from school on the Monday that Mr MacRae also became alarmed. Clearly, something had happened to her and, with this realization, his wife's friend, Mrs Valerie Steventon, felt obliged to reveal not only the fact that Mrs MacRae had a married lover with whom she had planned to spend the weekend – but also his identity.

When Mr MacRae, a director of a building firm, learned to his dismay that 'the other man' who had been having an affair of four years' duration with his wife was his own company secretary, William MacDowell, the unmasked lover was promptly dismissed. At this difficult time, the latter's embarrassment was doubtless compounded by a required admission of his clandestine affair also to the police; but he told them he had been at home all weekend after the 'tentative arrangement' to spend the days with Mrs MacRae had fallen through.

Meanwhile, after setting up a range of floodlights around the lay-by at Dalmagarry, officers began an intensive search for any clue left after a weekend of heavy rain. The car was taken to headquarters for forensic examination and, as Mrs MacRae's friend had mentioned that it had been giving some trouble, a BMW technician was flown up from Glasgow in an attempt to establish whether or not the car had been deliberately set on fire. Although these tests were inconclusive, there was that one small clue in the boot …

The priority at this stage, however, was to find both Mrs MacRae and Andrew – later revealed to have been fathered by MacDowell – dead or alive; and a massive search was launched into the wild terrain and bitter winter weather around the north's biggest town. It involved the intense combing of hundreds of square miles by police, army, civilian volunteers, tracker dogs, sub-aqua teams, RAF aircraft and civilian helicopters. Even the floorboards of Mrs MacRae's own bungalow (where she had been seen by a workman at about 4 p.m. on the Friday) were pulled up, and the foundations exhaustively searched. And at one point, a mechanical digger, ironically borrowed from Mr MacRae's building business, delved – without success – into a quarry once used during realignment and reconstruction of the A9 around the lay-by area. This led to local speculation that the bodies of the mother and son had ended up encased in concrete from the building work … a rather fanciful notion perhaps, though it was 'not discounted' by the officers involved in the search.

Yet no concrete evidence, literal or metaphorical, was forthcoming from their wide-ranging efforts in the field. Dozens of disused, water-filled quarries and tips were examined, every possible lead checked out. They brought in a hypnotist to probe witnesses' minds more deeply, and even followed up a claim by a spiritualist that she could pinpoint the separate burial-places of the mother and child after receiving messages from Mrs MacRae with the aid of a Ouija board. Several hundred people, including all the members of the staff at Mr MacRae's building firm in the town's Harbour Road industrial estate, were interviewed – and produced, among other things, two reports that Mrs MacRae had been seen travelling in her car with an unidentified, moustachioed man in Inverness the night before her disappearance; and another report which referred to a man seen standing by a parked car about 200 yards from the lay-by where, about two hours later, Mrs MacRae's car was seen in flames.

Although the latter man eventually came forward – a German-based serviceman who was interviewed for the police by military authorities – neither he nor any other interviewees yielded any leads, despite a £1,000 reward for information offered by Mr MacRae. With such a paucity of evidence and witnesses, the mystery became foggier by the day. And the only clue remained the one found in the car …

There were, however, plenty of theories, and Chief Constable Henderson himself put forward no fewer than five: that Mrs MacRae had deliberately absented herself from home for her own reasons; that she and the child had somehow had an accident; that she had taken her own (and the child's) life; that they had been murdered by someone who was known to her; or that they had been murdered by someone unknown to her.

The fact was, he pointed out, that the 37-year-old mother had given two different people two different reasons for going away. The last positive sighting was at her husband's office at five that night, five hours before her car was found ablaze; and 'from that moment on, there was neither sight nor sound of the woman'.

That there had been no sight of her was unquestionably true; but the matter of sound had earlier been intriguingly challenged by her self-confessed lover, a father of two teenage children within his own marriage, who claimed that twice during Mrs MacRae's first missing weekend his telephone had rung with the secret signal arrangement he and she had employed for the four years of their affair; he added that the police had even been present during the second 'call' – and his wife Rosemary, standing by his side despite his revelations, later expressed surprise that they had claimed to be unaware of this.

The implication was that Mrs MacRae had simply run away with her son and was trying to get a message through to her lover that they were all right. Which remains, of course, a possible scenario. Although one would still wonder why her car had to go up in flames, it might be reasonable to ask: had Mrs MacRae finally decided to call it a day and put some time and distance between her and the obvious stresses of a clandestine relationship that looked unlikely ever to achieve the relative dignity of openness? This idea could be tentatively upheld by the fact that detectives who searched her ranch-style bungalow – where she had gone to live with her sons just a mile from Mr MacDowell's home – found that she had been in the process of packing household goods and children's toys into tea-chests as if planning to leave quite soon.

Yet the theory could also lend support to quite another

scenario put forward by her friend, Mrs Steventon, to whom she had confided many details of her otherwise-secret, long-standing affair. Apparently, the missing woman had spoken of a forthcoming move to live permanently with her lover in Shetland; it was alleged that she even had the room measurements of the oil-company house which she said was waiting for them. But the existence of such a plan was not acknowledged by Mr MacDowell who, a week after the disappearances, emphatically denied to the press that there had been any such job, house, or intention.

So could Mrs MacRae have taken her own life, and Andrew's, to put an end to what Chief Constable Henderson called 'her difficulties'? The elementary objection to that theory is the absence of bodies: it would be practically impossible to commit suicide and perfectly hide away one's own corpse, not to mention someone else's, at the same time. And a similar objection – why no bodies? – must also apply to the 'accident' theory.

Was it, therefore, murder? Despite, or perhaps even because of, the absence of bodies, the now-late Chief Constable Henderson himself never concealed his personal conviction, that that was the case. And there was always that one clue from the car that served to strengthen his belief …

Although they could not establish whether or not the mother and son perished in the blazing car, or indeed ascertain the cause of the fire which had obliterated all fingerprints and other possible evidence inside it, forensic scientists made a discovery that suggested physical injury with some connection to it: in the boot there were minute traces of blood which were later found to be of the same group as that of Mrs MacRae and Andrew. It was quite possible, of course, that the blood represented evidence only of some minor scratch sustained in an innocent task – such as the fetching of tools or the removal of a spare wheel – but it was equally possible that it represented something more sinister by far. Simply: had the bodies of

Mrs MacRae and her son been at some point secreted in the car's boot? And the presence of the blood in the car was almost as interesting to detectives as the absence of other things: where were the clothes, holdall, handbag, and blue canvas pushchair that Mrs MacRae was known to have taken from her house? Could the buggy have been used to transport the bodies?

In any case, these facts strongly suggested to the police the involvement of at least one other person. Had Mrs MacRae been with someone in the 'blank' five-hour period between being seen at her husband's office and the time of the car-blaze? If so ... who? And had this person been her killer? Had she and the boy been murdered in the car or elsewhere and later driven, in the boot, to the lay-by for disposal? If so, where did their remains disappear to? Was the car later deliberately set alight to destroy all potential evidence? Or had the 'troublesome' vehicle burst into flames by itself causing the mother and child to flee from it ... only to be picked up by an ostensibly-helpful passing driver who abducted them? If so, why would the escaping Mrs MacRae, with child in arms, have wasted vital time in locking the car? To this day, the questions go on and on and the case remains, as Donald Henderson put it, 'a most peculiar mystery'.

The Renee MacRae file remains open, however, as the police still get letters and verbal approaches claiming to reveal fresh information and leads. All of them are checked out – at the time of writing, there was still one officer permanently assigned to the case at Inverness – and, as recently as November 1987, some 'new information' received prompted police to speak again to Mr MacDowell 'as we have done many times in the past years'. Speaking for Mr MacDowell – who spent several years working for a construction company in the Middle East after the case hit the headlines – Inverness solicitor Michael Sangster said his client 'was surprised to be asked the same questions as before. It was upsetting for the family and he was puzzled that police didn't tell him anything new. They just dealt with the same questions as they did eleven years ago'.

Gordon MacRae has now rebuilt his life, having divorced the missing Renee in 1980 and remarried the following year. Five years later, his new wife, Vivienne, gave birth to a daughter, Claire Louise, and he is still director of the building firm he and his brother built up from a family joinery business. But he finds it hard to forget the traumatic events of 1976, and says: 'Though the bodies of Renee and Andrew have never been found, there is no doubt in my mind that they were murdered. I have views on what must have happened but I have no way of proving them. I just wish that some new development would finally close the curtain forever.'

That is also the fervent wish of the current Chief Constable at Inverness, Hugh MacMillan, who seems confident that the riddle will eventually be solved. 'Our enquiry is far from over,' he says, 'as people keep coming forward with snippets of information and thoughts that they did not consider to be of value at the time. We take them all seriously, even people who claim to have seen things in trances. And you never know ... one day, someone might just walk in and say: "I did it". We are assuming, of course, that it was a matter of murder, but we cannot be certain until one or both of the bodies are found.'

How would such a discovery help? 'Well, we do not even know for sure that these people are dead and, if we were to know, it could mean that certain relevance could be given to particular evidence already in our hands. The type of death and enlightenment on how and where it occurred could also be very helpful to the ultimate resolution of the case.'

There is always the outside possibility, of course, that Mrs MacRae and her son could be alive and well and living in some foreign land where they have built for themselves a new and less complicated existence. But the police know instinctively that this is highly unlikely. At one time or another over the years, a missing mother's love will cause a telephone to ring, a message somehow to be understood, a presence to be felt. And since that fateful weekend, there has been nothing.

Only silence.

13 Four Unforgotten Lives,
1977-83

Despite Glasgow's clever eighties campaign to whitewash
away its once-unfortunate 'No Mean City' image of urban
deprivation, the old reputations of – and contrasts
between – the two great cities of the East and West remain
indelibly fixed in the minds of many Scots not easily
impressed by cosmetic public relations exercises. For
them, the European City of Culture for 1990 is still the
tatty and tough capital of violent crime, where warm
hearts and cold steel sit uncomfortably together; and
Edinburgh remains the aloof, genteel city whose
unemotional, high-minded people are painfully slow to
make friends and equally unbothered about making
enemies, far less stabbing anyone in the back.

None of these images is quite accurate, of course; it
could never be so black-and-white. And indeed, despite its
physical grandeur and elegant façades, Edinburgh is not,
as it would like to think, far above the fray. Outside its
tourist-attracting centre of gleaming turrets and spires and
sophisticated shopping, there are many deprived areas
that breed quick-tempered men of violence, petty
criminals, and junkies; where AIDs is rife and graffiti-
covered shops boarded up. From such places, loud-
mouthed invaders often lay siege to unsuspecting people
on city-centre streets, in shopping arcades, on buses. A
recent case, for instance, suggested that it is not a good
idea to point out to such people that smoking is banned in
certain parts of a bus: for one man who did, the result was

a quick, almost fatal, disfiguring knife-slash accompanied by an ugly curse from a fast-disappearing shadow.

It therefore follows, almost inevitably, that on any Scottish map of violent crime, 'genteel' Edinburgh has to take its place alongside 'rough' Glasgow. And although some might contend in the eastern city's defence that this underlying volatility is a peculiarly modern phenomenon rooted in the frustration of post-war unemployment and television's bad influence, Scotland's 'respectable' capital cannot easily get off the historical hook either. Concentrating only on the period from Waterloo in the late 1920s, it would be possible to write a book about the city's many infamous murderers – and the distinguished author Allan Massie has done just that. Even leaving aside Burke and Hare, the most notorious of them all, his *Ill Met by Gaslight* chronicles five bloodcurdling cases that paint yesterday's Edinburgh, too, in the unlikely colours of turbulence and passion. But what all these cases had in common – from wild David Haggart's impulsive murder of a prison turnkey in the early nineteenth century to Donald Merrett's series of botched family murders well into the twentieth century – was an identified suspect.

What distinguishes some of the more recent murders in and around the city is the police's dispiriting failure, despite their intense and continuing employment of modern detection techniques, to bring the guilty parties to justice. Three separate incidents involving the deaths of four young girls between 1977 and 1983 have consistently baffled the police and troubled the local press – particularly the Edinburgh *Evening News* which, despite the passing of the years, still keeps the cases in the public eye with regular updates on the slightest developments. These four young lives – of Helen Scott, Christine Eadie, Susan Maxwell and Caroline Hogg – may be gone; but they will never be forgotten, either by their constantly-reminded communities or by the tenacious officers charged with tracking down the evil culprits who so cruelly took them.

For practical reasons, the cases have essentially been compressed into two investigations, although the police have been careful to keep open the possibility that similarities suggesting a common perpetrator in the Hogg and Maxwell cases could be only coincidental. They are quite certain, however, that the deaths of Helen Scott and Christine Eadie, both seventeen years old at the time, were linked …

The girls' shared ordeal that was to end so tragically began with a happy Saturday night out at the crowded World's End pub on the corner of St Mary's Street and the historic Royal Mile which stretches from the heights of the city's famous castle down to Holyrood Palace, the Queen's Scottish residence. The date was 15 October 1977. As they enjoyed the boisterous company, Helen and Christine – close friends since their schooldays – little suspected they would have only a few hours to live.

Swept along by the convivial atmosphere and being perhaps a little naîve in the ways of the world, they accepted the offer of drinks from two male strangers – in whose company they were later seen to leave the bar. That was about 11 p.m. The girls were never seen alive again.

The following day, Christine's body – battered about the head, stripped and sexually molested, with her hands tightly tied behind her back – was found on the foreshore of Gosford Bay between the East Lothian villages of Longniddry and Aberlady, about fourteen miles from the capital. And just two hours later, Helen's body was discovered in a similar condition six miles away in a stubble field near Haddington.

It was not surprising that, in the beginning, the police felt reasonably confident about their chances of finding the two male suspects, for not only had there been no serious attempt to hide the bodies – suggesting that their disposal had been rather careless, if not done in an alcoholic haze – but the World's End pub had been so busy the previous night that there must have been dozens of witnesses available to give descriptions of the men. But, to their surprise, detectives encountered a mystifying silence. Most people who had been in the pub that night must have known about the murder hunt which received nationwide publicity, but for whatever reason, most of them decided not to come forward and little valuable information was gleaned from the few who did. To this day, police believe that someone who was at the pub that night must know more, and could still volunteer the vital clue which could lead them to the killers.

At one point, it looked as if detectives might make some headway with the help of an anonymous, badly-spelled letter received during the height of their investigations. The writer, claiming to know who had killed the girls, wrote: 'We heard two men talking about the murders they commited because the girls would not give in to them. If you want we will go to the police in Edinburgh and we don't want our names mentioned.' But the writer of this cryptic message did not come forward, despite police appeals for him or her to do so.

It had the effect, however, of strengthening suspicions that the girls had been taken – probably to a city flat – in the hope of sexual gratification and that their refusal to co-operate had led, firstly, to their being raped and, secondly, to their being permanently silenced to protect the culprits from morning-after prosecution. The bodies would then have been driven to East Lothian and dumped in the remote spots where they were found.

The hunt for the guilty men was one of the biggest ever mounted in Scotland, with more than 20,000 statements taken and hundreds of potential leads followed up. Even the notorious Yorkshire Ripper, Peter Sutcliffe, was questioned at one stage. There was a forlorn hope that, as forensic evidence suggested only one of the two presumed abductors had strangled the girls while the other probably looked on with some distaste, the less violent partner-in-crime might eventually yield to a nagging conscience and break his silence.

It was not to be. But as late as 1988, there was new hope

that the fast-developing technique of genetic fingerprint-
ing – which matches biological specimens from a crime to
the blood, semen or hair of a suspect with astonishing
accuracy – could make a vital contribution to the eventual
identification of the killer or killers. And with no shortage
of samples to go on from the World's End case, the only
elements that remained missing were the elusive names to
match them to ...

The same perplexing problem was, at the time of writing,
keeping the Susan Maxwell and Caroline Hogg cases open
after many years of intense, computer-aided investigation.
It all began on the afternoon of Friday 30 July 1982, when
the pretty, 11-year-old Susan was making her way home
from tennis courts in the quiet Border town of Coldstream,
forty miles south of Edinburgh. Many people in passing
cars must have noticed the child in her yellow shorts and
T-shirt, swinging her tennis-racquet happily as she
walked the two-and-a-half miles towards her parents'
farmhouse. But she was never to reach it. Just after she
crossed the old stone bridge carrying the A697 over the
River Tweed, she vanished.

After two weeks of unbearable anguish for her family,
her body was found in a copse next to a lay-by on the A518
between Uttoxeter and Stafford, suggesting that she had
been abducted and killed by a driver travelling south. As
the police launched into exhaustive and urgent investigations, her death aroused outrage all over Britain. And it
had hardly subsided by one degree when the same thing
happened again ...

Almost exactly a year later, on the evening of 8 July 1983,
five-year-old Caroline Hogg dressed in her best lilac-
checked gingham dress – ran out of her home to play on
Edinburgh's Portobello Promenade where a funfair was a
magnetic attraction to many local children. It was a
distance of only 150 yards, but she never came home
again. Like Susan, she simply disappeared; and ten
anxiety-racked days later, her body was found in deep

grass next to a lay-by on the A444 near Twycross, Leicestershire, only thirty miles from the first gruesome discovery. In neither case was the cause of death properly established.

Deeply distressed by the terrible fate that had befallen their much-loved children, the two sets of parents reacted in very different ways to the media attention that suddenly focused in on them: the Hoggs moved house and retreated into a seclusion that would thwart reporters, while the Maxwells, both journalists themselves, poured their hearts out to their press colleagues – 'We needed them as much as they needed us,' said Susan's mother, Liz – in the hope, initially, that publicity would help find their daughter, and latterly, that it would be instrumental in bringing her killer to justice.

It seemed likely, too, that if the culprit ever did surface, it would turn out to be the same person who had killed Caroline, for many of the circumstances surrounding both girls' abductions were remarkably similar. Apart from the final neighbouring locations of their bodies, both girls disappeared on a Friday in July, and from roughly the same part of the country; a sexual motive is believed to have existed in both cases; both were pretty and smartly dressed; and both were found on the southbound side of the road, suggesting that their abductor was a driver who regularly travelled in the north but came home to the south.

So similar were the cases, in fact, that the police decided to merge them into a joint manhunt, the most intense ever launched in Britain. This certainly implied that on balance they believed the one-killer theory held the weight of probability, although they were consistently at pains to stress this was not a totally unquestioned assumption. It was, after all, just conceivable that the similarities were coincidental, and even possible that someone of sick and perverse mind, having read about the first case, might wish to tease and confuse investigators by perpetrating a copy-cat version of it …

It was felt, however, that the abductor might well have acted on impulse. Witnesses reported seeing Caroline Hogg in the company of a scruffy, unshaven man around the Portobello's seaside Fun City; and in Susan's case, people recalled seeing her trying to wrest her tennis-racquet from the hand of someone who had drawn up beside her in a car. What kind of a car? Descriptions were hazy, but new hope came from a spotlighting of the Maxwell-Hogg cases on the BBC's *Crimewatch UK* programme, which invites viewers to call up if they have any relevant information about crimes. The mention of a maroon Morris Marina produced several more witnesses; and other callers gave potentially useful information about found tennis-racquets and plastic flasks of the type Susan was carrying when she disappeared. In Caroline's case, there were encouraging responses prompted by descriptions of her missing clothing, and others that reported sightings of a man depicted in a police photofit.

Some callers suggested they knew the identity of an elusive 'Alice' who wrote two tantalizing, un-addressed letters from Dundee about a suspicious man she met on the day of Caroline's abduction. But, despite their immediate action on these tips and others – like the sighting of a distressed 'Caroline' in the back of a blue car near Coldstream – police have, to this day, made no significant progress in either case.

They are determined, however, not to be beaten. Several years into the hunt, a senior officer in Edinburgh vowed: 'He needn't think he's going to get away with it. We'll find him in the end if it takes us years.' And indeed their ongoing UK-wide commitment remains impressive. Along with Lothian and Borders police, many English forces are still involved in the hunt – notably Staffordshire, Leicestershire, Northumbria, and West Yorkshire, whose Bradford-based child murder bureau is linked by computer to the massive memory of a terminal in Edinburgh which has processed an unbelievable mountain of data ... details of 130,000 people who have been investigated; 50,000 statements from questioned suspects, alibi-supporters, and witnesses; 100,000 vehicles similar to the types seen at or near the sites of the disappearances; and 36,000 individual enquiries. 'What we hope,' added the Edinburgh officer, 'is that one day we will pick up someone for something trivial and all the little details will link up.'

When in April 1987, Northumbrian police unexpectedly arrested and began questioning a thirty-seven-year-old former travelling salesman as a suspect for the Maxwell-Hogg abductions – an initially sensational development reported in the largest, most lurid headline types the Scottish papers could find – it looked for a moment as if that vital link might have been made at last. But fifty-three hours later, as the director of public prosecutions ruled that there was insufficient evidence to justify criminal proceedings, the man, from Blyth, Northumberland, was free to go ... and voluntarily re-entered a psychiatric hospital where he had previously been a patient.

Under the overall command of Deputy Chief Inspector Hector Clark, based in Edinburgh but a regular twice-a-week visitor to the Bradford nerve-centre, the tenacious, long-suffering manhunters went back to their computer screens ... back to endless hours of fruitless data-checking ... back to the search for new ideas ... back to following up letters from mediums and people claiming to have dreamt details of the cases. For no angle, however cranky, could be left unexamined. In an attempt to enhance their recall, witnesses were even hypnotized by police doctors. All to no avail ...

Despite this frustrating absence of a breakthrough over the lengthening passage of time, the Edinburgh-based force still commits permanent manpower to the combined enquiry, with one officer working on it exclusively north of the Border and another based in the main incident room in Bradford. As Hector Clark has said:

> We admit that we are not making real progress, though every possible lead is being investigated; but the fact that we are still doing so after so many years is an indication of

the efforts the police service as a whole is putting into these tragic offences. Generally speaking, murder investigations are wound down after about twelve months, but we owe it to the parents of these children to look at every opportunity of finding who was responsible.

And to quote another, less senior, officer involved: 'When do you let go? The level of manning on a case like this might go up and down – but the answer is never. We can never let go until the culprit is found.'

If and when he is caught and brought to justice – and the police are virtually certain the perpetrator of each crime is a male – Susan's mother does not know how she will react: 'When I think about the man who did it, I'm in favour of capital punishment … Why should Susie lose her life and he go on living? But much as I'd like to see this person caught, I dread it. If he were to be found, a face and a name would be put to my horror. There would be a court case and it would all be dug up again.'

Not that she has ever managed to forget the tragic fate of her daughter for more than a day at a time, so deep is her sorrow. And she expresses it in ten simple, touching words that sum up the unforgivable outrage of such life-robbery: 'Susie and I could have been such good friends now …'

But the last, determined words must go to Hector Clark:

Though it is probably pointless, after all this time, to try to jog most people's memories, I am certain that there is someone somewhere in this country who, at the time these offences were committed, had grave suspicions about a father, a son, a brother, or some like person, and failed to report these to the police. Those suspicions must remain and I would urge that person to come forward, even at this late stage.

14   Who Fired the Gun?, 1985

He was something of a bulldog to look at, with dense, well-combed hair and deep-set eyes over a wry smile and Churchillian chin. But with more of a terrier's spirit; for, once he set his teeth into a target, William McRae simply would not let go. Ebullient and forceful, he was a man at once both feared and loved, a clever lawyer and one of the Scottish Nationalist Party's most memorable characters. Even the closest of his many friends could be taken aback by his passion and chosen causes ... by the often-unlikely avenues down which he drove his intellectual brilliance and dynamism. And he could make his opponents even less comfortable. His devastating and much-too-articulate frankness made him no friend, for instance, of certain sections of the British establishment against which he railed for much of his richly-textured bachelor life.

But on the night of Friday 5 April 1985 – or perhaps early the next morning – that 61-year-old life of many dimensions abruptly met the beginning of its mysterious end at a bleak and lonely place on the A87 Invergarry to Kyle of Lochalsh road: one of the few spots in rural Inverness-shire that is more sinister than picturesque; where the landscape is angular and rocky and casts lifeless shadows, with no trees and little green. The perilous, narrow road on which he had been driving to his holiday crofthouse near Loch Duich, Ross-shire, plunges steeply down on the left-hand side through dry-brown heather and scree to the faraway shore of Loch Loyne. A road on which the most reckless of drivers would go slowly for fear of meeting another vehicle coming the other way. But one way or another, this evil road claimed William McRae after one of its slower bends, in what at first looked like an unfortunate accident ...

By a strange coincidence, the inquiry into the Atomic Energy Authority's controversial plan for a new reprocessing plant at Dounreay was to open exactly one year later. And after his 'accident' some suspicious minds suggested that certain establishment hearts might not have been gladdened to learn that this most active of human-rights activists was planning to participate in it; for his headline-grabbing words at a previous, similar hearing in 1980 – at which he represented the SNP in its opposition to proposed test drilling for nuclear waste sites in Ayrshire's Mullwharchar Hills – would not be easily forgotten.

'Nuclear waste,' he said then among other stinging comments, 'should be stored where Guy Fawkes put his gunpowder.'

The media loved it. His opponents flinched. And there was no doubt that, given half a chance, he would deliver more such telling rhetorical blows at Dounreay. But empty rhetoric wasn't his style. There would have to be substance to it. Was he getting his terrier's teeth into such substance as he set off on that Good Friday evening from his small office in Buchanan Street, Glasgow, taking with him certain files to study over the Easter break? No one knows for sure, but friends who saw him leave recalled that he was bubbling with enthusiasm as he called out excitedly: 'I've got them! I've got them!'

Those cryptic words were as puzzling then as they are now, for they were never to be elaborated upon by William McRae. The next morning, with three-quarters of his journey behind him, his damaged Volvo was found – about seventy yards off the road, down the rough incline facing the loch – by a passing Australian tourist who, thoroughly shaken, flagged down the first car that came along. As fate would have it, the driver was another SNP

member, Dundee councillor David Coutts, on his way to
Skye for a family holiday. When he looked inside the
wrecked car, he was shocked to recognize Mr McRae in
the driving seat, still precariously hanging on to life in a
state of coma, with bloody head injuries.

An ambulance quickly summoned, he was rushed to
hospital in Inverness and then transferred to Aberdeen,
where he died early the following morning. The morning
after that, his obituary in *The Scotsman* began with the
following sentence, which suggested simple acceptance of
death by car-crash injury:.

> ... Mr William McRae died yesterday in Aberdeen Royal
> Infirmary after a car accident in the Highlands.

Seven more paragraphs outlined his biography, his many
achievements and occasional disappointments – including
his failure, three times, to be elected SNP Member of
Parliament for Ross and Cromarty – and that might simply
have been that. But two weeks later the bombshell burst
... when it was officially revealed that his death had been
caused by a .22 bullet wound to the head.

Despite his friends' protestations that McCrae was the
last person in the world who would contemplate such a
thing, the initially-accepted assumption by the authorities
and the general public was that he must have inflicted the
fatal injury upon himself, must have decided to commit
suicide in this dark and isolated spot where he knew there
would be no witnesses; he was, after all, known to possess
a .22 revolver. But, strange to tell, no information about
the ownership of the twice-fired death weapon was
released. Even stranger, the information that did become
available later – particularly the fact that the gun was
found by police in a stream some twenty yards away from
what must have been the scene of the shooting – served
only to create more and more mystery. Indeed, with the
emergence of each new fact, doubt and suspicion grew
ever deeper, making official explanations increasingly
difficult to accept. Eventually, there seemed to be too

many anomalies in the case for the media and public to settle for the simple suicide assumption. For instance ...

Mr McRae had apparently been shot above the right ear, but there were no burns around the wound consistent with close-range self-infliction.

Another disturbing observation was made by Councillor Coutts who recalled that, when he came upon the crash scene, he found it 'peculiar that Mr McRae's watch, cheque cards and other personal effects were some way away from the car. A lot of things had been ripped up'.

The car's back window had been smashed too; and its ignition and door keys had been found on the dying man's lap.

Also puzzling was the absence of the victim's briefcase and/or files which he was known to have taken with him; they appeared to have vanished without trace. But most bewildering of all was the matter of the 'thrown-away' gun.

Whose hand had created these inconsistencies and disturbances? It is hard to believe it was that of William McRae who, if he had indeed shot himself in the head, would hardly have been in a fit condition to lob his suicide weapon twenty yards from the car in which he sat fatally wounded. The hand of a simple ransacking vandal perhaps, who had come upon the tragic scene later and tried to profit from it? Or could it have been ... and speculation was growing fast ... the sinister and expert hand of a long-range marksman who was also a cold-blooded killer?

There was, after all, no shortage of hostile reaction to McRae and many of his works; there were even, it was said, low-lying and resentful enemies with vengeful intent. Alongside the many other causes he championed, McRae had been a persistent campaigner in international circles for Scotland's own legal and constitutional rights. It was also said that he had connections with militant nationalist groups. Indeed, his personal and political history and geography were littered with controversy. He was a well-travelled man who at one moment would be flying to meet business commitments in the People's Republic of China, at another lecturing on maritime law at the University of Haifa, at yet another chatting sympathetically in Urdu with an Asian client in his small Glasgow office.

While much loved and respected by those in his corner, he was also undoubtedly perceived as an annoying, even dangerous, thorn in the flesh of more than a few others. So was someone, some agency, trying to remove the thorn once and for all? One suspicious sign was the mystery of a fire at his house the day before he died. Another was the very date of his fatal 'accident'. Was it merely a coincidence that 6 April was Scottish Independence Day – the anniversary of the 1320 Declaration of Independence at the Abbey of Arbroath? Or was it a deliberate signal being sent to the more zealous nationalists whose most fanatical faction, the Scottish National Liberation Army (SNLA), claimed to have come close to murdering the Prime Minister with a bomb attack on the 1983 Scottish Conservative conference in Perth?

The questions are easy to pose. The evidence and the answers are considerably more difficult to come by. To the central question, for example – who, specifically, would want to silence William McRae and why? – there are too many possible answers with very little beyond the circumstantial to support them; a positive plethora of hypotheses that range from the simplistic through the plain foggy to the utterly fanciful. In rising degrees of complexity, starting with supposed justifications for taking his own life, they went something like this …

— The rumour went round – and surely his friends didn't start it – that he was homosexual, which supposedly made him susceptible to emotional instability and perhaps even blackmail.

— Having been convicted in the past for driving over the legal alcohol limit, he was fearful, some said, of more shame. It was hinted that being on the brink of another such prosecution had made him apprehensive and depressed enough to take his own life.

— There were suggestions, allegedly based on his own statements, that McRae had been trying to help stamp out drug smuggling on the west coast of Scotland and had thus incurred the traffickers' displeasure, making himself an obvious target for a hitman.

— Because the proposed new reprocessing plant at Dounreay was of such supreme importance to the area in terms of employment, could there have been some local party who believed that a powerfully persuasive voice against it – such as McRae's – would be best pre-emptively silenced by fair means or foul?

— Some of the media suggested he was too close to the bellicose nationalist militants, which could mark him as an 'enemy of the state'. Indeed, a 1988 article in *Carn*, journal of the Celtic League, quoted the SNLA as claiming, in a clandestine newspaper, that McRae had been 'an active sympathiser' who had assisted them financially as well as in planning attacks; the SNLA had also accused the British state 'of the murder of Willie McRae and of attempting a crude and ineffective cover-up'.

— And finally, a correspondent to *The Scotsman* suggested that the lawyer could also have been regarded as an 'enemy of the state' for more historical reasons. Alan Clayton, a one-time fellow-member of the SNP's strategy committee which often met at McRae's Glasgow office, wrote that, while McRae was with the British Army in India between 1945 and 1947, he maintained a clandestine contact with the Indian National Congress 'and it was due to this "early warning system" that an illegal and peripatetic liberation radio station operating around the New Delhi area was able to stay one step ahead of the British Army during the liberation struggle.

'Such activity, of course, rendered him liable to the

firing squad. British security was unable to prove these activities, but neither did it forgive or forget ...' After several other allegations of activity liable to upset the British establishment, Clayton concluded: 'To my mind it is abundantly clear that William McRae was a well-established, dangerous and deadly enemy of a State which will go to apparently any lengths to sustain and protect itself.'

These ideas were promptly countered by another letter-writer, James MacRae – 'a close friend from 1940 onward, particularly during his university career' – who pointed out that William McRae had been an officer in the Royal Indian Navy (not the British Army) and that by 1947 he was 'well into his law degree course, having resumed his studies on the same day as I, in October, 1946'. He went on: 'I know that at the time his sympathies were more with Pakistan than India. In any case, why "clandestine" contact with the Indian National Congress? When I left the Far East in September, 1946, the establishment of Indian independence was generally regarded as an imminent certainty. A well-established, dangerous and deadly enemy of the state? No, no, Mr Clayton, I cannot accept that.' He ended with a plea that his friend be allowed to rest in peace.

But considering the undying strength of the controversy, it seemed most unlikely that William McRae would be allowed such a posthumous luxury

Although a good deal of that controversy – and the popular theorizing outlined above – took place two or three years after the original incident, many nagging questions had already arisen within months of it and, to try to set them to rest, the pressure inevitably mounted for a fatal accident inquiry. At first, the chances of one being set up looked promising. Although the procurator fiscal at Inverness, Thomas Aitchison, had initially said there were no suspicious circumstances to merit such an inquiry, he conceded in mid-June of 1985 that 'that was before other matters were raised; now all sorts of factors are coming into this'. He also admitted that the Crown Office in Edinburgh had asked him to continue inquiries after he submitted his original report on the death. And the Solicitor General, Peter Fraser, agreed that if there were any real degree of public concern about the circumstances of the death, he would be 'prepared to consider' a fatal accident inquiry.

But to the astonishment of the many interested parties, the Crown Office announced a little over two weeks later – roughly three months after McRae's death – that there was to be no inquiry. Its statement said that a full report on the death had been considered and Crown counsel were satisfied that there were no circumstances to warrant criminal proceedings or public inquiry.

The two men who had fought most vigorously for the probe-that-was-not-to-be were Bob McTaggart, Labour MP for McRae's constituency, and Councillor Coutts, who had first recognized his unfortunate colleague in the wreck of his car. In his campaign, McTaggart had declared: 'I just want to get to the bottom of this. If Willie McRae committed suicide it was a very strange way of doing it ... it just doesn't gel with me ... I would like some answers and I would like to see a public inquiry.' Both men's subsequent quiet, if reluctant, acceptance of the negative official decision seemed strange at first; then it became clear that they were respecting the wishes of the dead man's family – his next-of-kin was his brother, Dr Fergus McRae – who, said the Solicitor General, wished to see no further inquiries. And a letter from the Crown Agent dated 22 July stated flatly that 'no further information on the circumstances of this death will be made public'.

If it were hoped that this would finally put speculation to rest, however, that hope was clearly too optimistic. The mystery refused to lie dead and buried with William McRae. Doubts persisted and the SNP, anxious to quieten some of its louder voices on the subject, set up its own investigation headed by the party's widely-respected stateswoman, Winnie Ewing – not only a lawyer herself but also Euro-MP for the Highlands and Islands.

In the course of her inquiries, Mrs Ewing contacted a close friend and political associate of McRae, Michael Strathern – despite, or perhaps because of, the fact that he had been expelled from the SNP for being a member of the proscribed direct-action group Soil nan Gaidhael (Seed of the Gael). 'Many of us had hoped,' she wrote to him, 'that Willie could lie undisturbed but it appears that ... the Press will not let this happen.' She added a list of no fewer than thirty-three questions that she reckoned had not been satisfactorily resolved. Strathern's response welcomed her inquiry because those questions – covering the time of death, state of the car and personal effects, the police and procurator fiscal's investigations, and the gun and the bullet – were the very ones he and others had been trying to get the Crown authorities to answer. In the kind of colourful language that would have delighted his late friend, he added the observation:

'From the beginning of this strange tale I have had a powerful sense of the presence of Willie McRae standing at my shoulder and declaring in far-from-dulcet tones, "For God's sake do something about it".' Nor did Strathern mince his words to the press. He had, he said, tried hard to see the incident as suicide but all the facts spoke against that explanation, as did McRae's character. 'He had so much still to do. If it had been the day after Scotland had won independence, his work would have been done and I might have believed it. But all the facts speak against it being suicide. And the claim by the Solicitor General and the Crown Agent that there were no suspicious circumstances is too preposterous for serious consideration and must give rise to suspicion in itself.'

Ewing made her move. Almost two years after the incident happened, she applied for access, as a lawyer, to the procurator fiscal's official papers relevant to the case. The idea was that, in the anticipated negotiations, she would offer an undertaking of confidentiality if, on reading the material, she accepted that there were no suspicious circumstances. In other words, if she felt the evidence did indeed point to suicide, the SNP would no longer pursue the matter. But in the event there were to be no negotiations. She was promptly rebuffed – a blunt statement from the Crown Office said previous requests had been turned down and there was no reason to think a new request would be treated differently – and to the surprise of many who were following the case, the party then appeared to give up without a fight; all it could officially do was 'regret' that decision.

Though it certainly looked as if she had backed down reluctantly, Mrs Ewing would make no further comment on the case; but the surprised, bitter disappointment in some of the more-zealous nationalist circles was not confined to the same grudging resignation. They began to suggest openly that Mrs Ewing had learned something, somehow, in the course of her inquiry that had had the effect of cooling its intensity. The inevitable elaboration was to allege that – militancy being perceived by voters as a negative factor in a political party's electability – McRae had been disowned by the SNP hierarchy for the same reason that he had been murdered by the security forces: that he was too close to those prepared to resort to force for the nationalist cause.

Could there conceivably be anything in that? It seemed appropriate to ask the chairman of the party, Gordon Wilson. He said:

> There may have been some mystery about Willie's death, but there was no mystery about the end of our inquiry. There was simply a limit to what could be done. We would have liked access to the papers, of course, but there was no legal precedent for such a procedure and, having decided it was suicide and having made the no-inquiry decision, the authorities were then just immobilised by their own bureaucracy. Once decisions had been made, they couldn't be changed.
>
> But it's important to remember that, at the very

beginning, before the relatives made their feeling clear – that they believed it was suicide – the authorities had not been unwilling to consider an inquiry. In fact, the Solicitor General even approached me at the time to ask if the party wanted one. I spoke to the relatives and they said they'd be very upset if there were one.

But, speaking hypothetically, would the party have found a sympathy between McRae and the direct-action zealots unpalatable? 'Well, are there any such advocates of violence?' asked Wilson. 'The SNLA? Who are they? Do they even exist? Have you ever seen them, or any damage they've done? I certainly haven't. But if they did exist and if Willie had had connections with them, yes, the party would have found that slightly embarrassing; but no more than that. For latterly, he wasn't such an influential figure as he had been. He certainly could not be seen as representing the party's stance on anything. His influence had been greater in the Sixties and Seventies.'

So was the party boss saying that he saw nothing sinister in his death at all? 'I accept that there were a lot of questions that should have been answered publicly – though, after the passage of time, I doubt now whether they could be answered adequately – but my own feeling has always been that it was suicide. Willie had a lot of problems about which he could get depressed, not the least of them being his health.'

In Wilson's opinion, could there have been anything to the security-forces allegation? There were, after all, reports that McRae had claimed jubilantly to friends, in the days before his death, that he had made a breakthrough in his work that would soon have the Special Branch closing in on him ... 'It's always possible, of course, that it was a sinister action by officers of the British State, and after the SAS killings on Gibraltar, I'm almost willing to believe anything. Almost ... but I'd need to be convinced.'

Be that as it may, with his party's retirement from the ring, others felt the obligation to keep the McRae flame alight in a less official but more passionate way ... more in keeping, perhaps, with the individual campaigning spirit of the man. To pay their respects and express their displeasure at what they perceived as the inaction of the authorities, friends and other interested parties got the protest show on the road again – literally. The A87 road, where the Volvo had originally come to grief. They began an annual tradition of visiting the site of the incident – now marked with a cairn of rocks from various parts of Scotland – and speaking their minds into the biting wind.

When nearly one hundred of them first gathered in 1987 to erect the memorial cairn on an outcrop of rock high above Loch Loyne and not so far above what had been the scene of the crime-that-never-was, it seemed that Councillor Coutts had found his voice again as he joined other calls for more information on the affair. He recalled that, for that very purpose, he had contacted the Solicitor General, the Lord Advocate, and the procurator fiscal at Inverness 'and the wall of silence that has been put up suggested to me that some department has something to hide'.

With the magnificent, malevolent view across the loch stretching out behind him, a piper played a lament and a eulogy was given by Michael Strathern as the Scottish flag was raised after fluttering at half-mast on the nearby flagstaff. He spoke of William McRae as a great Scottish patriot who, like Martin Luther King, Gandhi and others, had lived with the constant threat of an assassin's bullet. And later, with unequivocal boldness, he said what was on the mind of everyone who had made the pilgrimage to that strangely sinister place: 'There was nothing suspicious about Willie's death – he was murdered, otherwise we wouldn't be here. I can think of two factions who would have wanted him dead.'

So who is right? It is not uncommon, of course, for those who hold strong political views to find their way through often-imaginary mazes to the kind of conclusion that others would consider unlikely at best. But, perhaps paradoxically, such exotic plants grow best on the thinnest of informational grounds. And there is no doubt that in this case more official enlightenment would have led to less public suspicion, less fanciful hypothesizing. Perhaps it is not too much to hope that the answers to at least some of the nagging, outstanding questions might yet be forthcoming. But until they are, it seems regrettable that the impartial observer of this perplexing mystery must make a simple choice between two highly unsatisfactory explanations for its existence: immobile bureaucracy or sinister conspiracy.

Ironically, perhaps the man best suited to blast open such a case would have been the sharp and colourful William McRae himself. A man who was unquestionably larger than life, and who is now – thanks in some measure to the system he challenged so energetically when he was alive – a good deal larger than death.

15   Little Boy Lost, 1988

For many people, the most immediate pleasure of being in Scotland is the easy access from towns and cities into the open, beautiful, and often empty countryside. From whatever urban centre you care to name, it is possible to make your way out of it within minutes rather than hours, to suddenly find yourself walking for miles through rugged, heather-carpeted hills without seeing another living soul. But this fact, which makes a holiday north of the border a refreshing prospect for visitors from more crowded countries, was not so kind to one little local holidaymaker in mid-September 1988 ... when, for the first time in his short life, 5-year-old Stephen McKerron went on a week's break from his home in Hamilton.

Not that his was to be that kind of away-from-it-all holiday. For weeks the cheerful, brown-haired lad had been excited about the prospect of seven days' non-stop fun at Butlins' Wonderwest holiday park in Ayr. Although only about forty miles lie between there and Hamilton, the sprawling seaside leisure complex with its jolly colours and roller-coaster thrills would be a surprisingly different world from the modest home environment of Donald Terrace young Stephen knew so well. He had never been away from his parents and two younger brothers before, but he would be in the good and loving hands of his aunt and uncle, Lyn and Ian Sneddon, who thought the world of him. And like any hard-working mother, Lyn's sister-in-law Janet would be glad of the brief respite from happily-accepted, but nonetheless tiring, demands of bringing up her most lively son.

It seemed like the perfect arrangement: a welcome change for everyone. But it was to last no more than a Saturday afternoon before it turned into a nightmare that threatened never to end. In fact, although they knew the memory of it would still haunt them forever, the worst of it lasted for fifteen dreadful days and nights – through which Stephen's desperately distraught relatives were deprived of sleep, news, even hope; fifteen days and nights in which every empathizing parent in the country prayed not only for them ... but also, and especially, for little Stephen.

For, only three hours after he enthusiastically launched himself into Wonderwest's exciting holiday atmosphere of inflatable castles, fun-rides, cafés, crowds, and lifesize cartoon characters, the adventurous little boy just vanished ... as if he had never existed. As his grandmother, Mrs Sheila McEwan, said later: 'You know what children are like. One minute they are by your side, and the next time you look, they are away.' It was almost exactly like that.

Being only twenty-three, and perhaps not yet very experienced in the wayward ways of children, Ian and Lyn Sneddon were caught out when each thought the other was watching young Stephen as he played on an escalator. Ian had gone down a parallel staircase to collect him, but by the time he reached the bottom, Stephen was halfway back up the escalator towards Lyn. She said later: 'By the time Stephen got down the stairs, Ian would have gone; and when he came back up, I was gone.' It was just a matter of seconds, but in that moment of confusion, each adult thought the youngster was with the other.

It was about 6 p.m. When they realized that Stephen was lost, Ian and Lyn started their own anxious hunt for the boy. With a rapidly-growing feeling of panic, they hurried around the complex, weaving in and out of the happy holidaymaking crowds, desperately asking anyone and everyone if they had seen him, searching every corner of the sprawling complex; but eventually, having exhausted every avenue, they realized with a chilling dread that Stephen was nowhere to be found … that he could even be outside the complex. At that moment, about 8.55 p.m., they informed the camp's security staff – who in turn immediately informed the police.

That alert set off Scotland's biggest-ever child hunt, with 200 officers initially checking 1500 chalets and caravans at the site. A description of Stephen was quickly circulated – three feet tall, dressed in a fawn T-shirt bearing the legend *Ready Steady Go*, blue tracksuit trousers, and grey training shoes – and first enquiries brought to light several presumed sightings of him both inside and outside the park. One report referred to such a boy being seen inside the Moonraker café-bar about half an hour after Stephen's disappearance; he was apparently 'distressed' and being comforted by a middle-aged man. Another witness had seen a young boy who answered Stephen's description climbing the seven-foot-high perimeter fence of the park that evening. But the reports given most credence by the police were those by motorists who said they had seen 'Stephen' walking away from the holiday camp in a southerly direction, along the side of the Ayr-Turnberry road at about 6.30 p.m. All vehicles leaving and approaching the holiday complex were systematically searched and drivers asked either to keep a look-out for the boy or try to remember something that might help: had anyone seen a car stopping, or a boy on the road, crossing the road, or in fields beside the road?

The police did not realize it at the time, but at this early point in their investigations the trail was quite warm. It went cold, it seems, because of the limits imposed on the search area. Yet the search was on a massive scale and covered a large area: a six-mile oval drawn around the leisure complex, even into the sea. In addition to the special squads of officers drafted in from other parts of Strathclyde to search the area on foot, divers were called in to check burns, rivers and water-tanks; coastguard services were enlisted to scan the shore and beyond; and to survey the hillsides, there was even a helicopter carrying heat-seeking equipment that could detect a body from afar. And then, of course, there were hundreds of civilian volunteers – including Stephen's parents – who helped the police comb dense vegetation, ditches and fields. But no further clue to the boy's whereabouts was found; no response to police appeals forthcoming. Slowly, reluctantly, the assumption began to take root that the boy had been abducted ...

With Stephen's parents now accommodated at the leisure complex and too upset to speak, his grandfather, Tucker McEwan, came forward to appeal to whoever might be holding him: 'I don't think he has gone wandering and I don't think he would go off with anyone willingly. I fear he may have been abducted and we can only hope and pray that he will come back safely.' But his touching plea had no material effect; and the silence of no reaction, of no news at all, became deafening.

The brief ray of a possible breakthrough came with the finding on a Midlothian roadside of a mysterious suitcase which contained, according to the first press reports, bloodstained clothing and personal papers that seemed to link its owner to Wonderworld. But this apparently sensational lead was quickly killed by the police after their enquiries revealed that the items were more innocent than they looked; that the clothing – a man's suit – had not in fact been stained with blood. And soon, they were compelled to concede that they were 'desperate' for any, more substantial leads. Among the immediate family, this admission created a feeling more chilling than would the worst of bad news; and the terrors of the imagination were taking the place of explanations. Where was the boy and what terrible things were happening to him? Was he being held in great distress by some sinister stranger whose emotionless, evil intent allowed him to shrug off the child's screams for his parents, and the family's anguish in their helplessness?

The extent of the anguish suffered by Stephen's parents and uncle and aunt, mercilessly blaming themselves, was to be seen on their tearful, sleepless, red-puffed faces when – to keep the newsless case in the public eye as the days began to turn into weeks – they faced the media together at an emotional press conference to appeal once again for their son's abductor to come forward. 'I just want him back,' said his 25-year-old mother in a shaking voice. 'He is just a normal wee boy. He would not run away, I know he would not run away. He was so excited about the holiday.' Pictures of the family appeared on virtually every newspaper front page and every television set in the land, and anyone but a recluse would have read or heard their plea and been moved by it; but still the only response was silence.

Were Stephen indeed being held against his will, it was of course clutching at straws to hope that his abductor would step forward when appealed to. Nevertheless, the lack of even peripheral leads from suspicious neighbours or workmates led the family to wonder: could they indeed be dealing with a recluse? Or perhaps with someone who travelled north but lived far beyond the reach of the Scottish media?

This latter possibility had already occurred to Strathclyde police, prompting them to consider setting up a computer link with the child murder bureau in West Yorkshire, headquarters for the inquiry into the notorious murders of Susan Maxwell and Caroline Hogg. A few years before, these two little girls had disappeared from south-east Scotland in circumstances that seemed similar to those surrounding Stephen's disappearance. Abducted on midsummer days of leisure, their bodies had eventually been found in the English Midlands, only thirty miles from each other. Could the same fate have befallen Stephen, as a victim of the same hand? But just before the link to the files and witness lists at Bradford could be effected, the news finally came that was to end the McKerrons' dreadful days and sleepless nights of waiting and wondering ...

Fifteen days after Stephen's disappearance, on the afternoon of Sunday 2 October, Lady Margaret MacLehose, the wife of the former governor of Hong Kong, was out exercising her dog on the hills near her home at Beoch, north of Maybole, when she came across the body of a little boy, huddled in an open, fenced ditch only about half a mile from two farmhouses. Her own house was only about a mile away and, not being the kind of lady to let shock get the better of her, she hurried back to it to raise the alarm.

It was soon confirmed that the body was Stephen's. He had apparently travelled the entire distance on foot – a total of six miles south along the coast road and inland into the Garrick Hills along a small hill road – and finally died of exposure. The hill road, which winds its way inland for about six miles to the town of Maybole, has a web of tracks leading off it into some of the most inhospitable country in south-west Scotland, and it was close to one of these tracks that the body was found. Tragically, it seemed that Stephen's own surprising strength in such a situation had brought about his own death. For the police had drawn the limits of their oval search-area at the furthest points they felt such a youngster could reach under his own power ... and Stephen's body was found just beyond its south-eastern limit.

It was tragic, too, that he was so close to help when he died, probably in the darkness of his first night in the rough hillside terrain: the kind of land he had probably never seen before. 'I know he was trying to get home to me', sobbed his mother when she heard the news. 'The thought of him lost and crying for me will live with me forever.' He could not possibly have reached his mother, of course; but if he had seen a beckoning light, perhaps he could have struggled on to one of the two nearby farmhouses – Glenalmond and Glenbay – or even to the MacLehoses' house.

'It's a tragedy,' said farmer Daniel Dunlop, of Glenalmond. 'He was so near to us. My wife and I were almost weeping when we were told the lad had been found dead in the field nearby. If he could just have staggered on a wee bit more, he might have seen our lights and made it to the farm.'

What puzzled many people was why the search area had been so restricted, when the helicopter-mounted heat-seeking equipment would have stood a good chance of finding him had its operators been given a wider brief. Police replied: 'How far do you go ... ten miles, twenty miles? We have long experience from similar previous searches and our area-limitation was based not only on that but on the advice of a consultant paediatrician; and bearing that in mind, we took into account the age of the boy, the weather, and the terrain.'

As Stephen's grieving family prepared for his funeral and a post-mortem confirmed that he had died of natural causes – 'He wasn't harmed in any way,' said Janet, 'he just curled up when he became exhausted and simply passed away in his sleep' – other people began to focus on the mystery of just how such a lightly-dressed and diminutive lad could have traversed by himself so much rugged terrain known to be difficult enough for fit, hill-walking adults. One of the doubters was his own grandfather, who, implying that he would like to see the police investigation continued, said: 'I don't believe Stephen could have gone all that distance on his own. I believe someone must have taken him there and left him to die.'

That was, of course, a possibility. It was conceivable that, as the confused little boy wandered away from Wonderwest, a passing driver might have stopped, picked him up, and driven him into the hills – perhaps with the altruistic motive of calming him down and finding out where he had come from before returning him safely; perhaps with a less laudable intent. But it was clear that Stephen had not been hurt; so had he – being taught, like most of today's children, not to trust strangers – panicked, jumped out of the car and fled into the rough terrain?

Certainly, he must have been driven by some urgent emotion to have gone so far. Howard Jefferson, a local official of the National Farmers' Union, expressed 'amazement' that the boy could have trekked that distance over what he described as 'hellish territory'. And farmer Dunlop commented: 'I was very surprised that he got half that distance in the countryside. The hills, the woods, marshlands, fences, drops into gullies and what have you … I don't know how he did it.' His doubts were echoed by a Glasgow child doctor who said it was 'very odd' that Stephen had managed to walk so far and confirmed that it was 'quite a distance for a five-year-old child'. And the *Daily Record* screamed across a centre-page spread,

SIX-MILE RIDDLE: HOW DID A LITTLE LAD
WALK SO FAR TO MEET HIS DEATH?

But a police spokesman said there was no evidence to suggest that Stephen had reached the location of his death by any means other than his own efforts; and nothing new had come to light that would justify a continuation of police investigations. Stephen's finder, Lady MacLehose, was also rather less puzzled by the boy's feat and found herself speaking out as an expert on that kind of country. 'I don't think it's that bad,' she said, 'I walked up there myself when I was about five years old and obviously I don't think it's impossible for a child to walk over that terrain. All right, it's heather, but one can walk over heather.'

Stephen's parents remained objective enough, however, to stay out of that controversy. 'Obviously,' said his father, 'when he first went missing, we feared the possibility of abduction; but we know now that is not what happened.' They also handled the matter of Lyn's anguished blaming of herself with considerable dignity. 'Of course we don't blame Lyn,' they said simply.

But the one question that haunted the McKerrons, as they stoically watched their son's little white coffin being lowered into his grave at Hamilton's rain-swept Bent cemetery – among wreaths from his school, his neighbours, and the place where his much-anticipated first holiday was never to be – was: how long after he disappeared did Stephen die? As doctors were unable to pinpoint that with any certainty, his parents could only hope fervently that he had not suffered for long. And knowing instinctively that the amazing power in Stephen's little legs had been simply the power of love, they hoped too that, after stumbling for hours through the heather and the cold to find his way home to them, perhaps he just dreamt he had made it, as he lay down to sleep for the last time.

Stephen's father, however, was not wholly convinced that the boy's death had been natural. He pointed out that, when found, Stephen's socks had been in his pocket. 'My wee boy couldn't tie his laces,' said Mr McKerron, who rejected the theory that his son would have wandered away from the holiday camp alone. 'My wife thinks he could have taken his socks off because they were wet and pulled his laced shoes on again; but I just don't believe he would have done that.'

He thus welcomed the news that a fatal accident inquiry was to be heard before Sheriff Neil Gow at Ayr. But its conclusions, delivered at the end of March 1989, were to offer little solace. Two other main theories were examined – that someone had taken the boy from outside the camp then left him, unharmed, in the hills to die; or that he had been killed by unknown means and his body subsequently dumped. But why not hidden? That question obviously bothered the sheriff …

In his twenty-one page judgment, he came down in favour of death by natural causes, with the simple conclusion that 'the enterprise and stamina of Stephen were seriously under-estimated by all concerned'. He thought it 'most likely that, in the terminal stages of exhaustion, Stephen simply collapsed in the ditch and passed away there shortly afterwards'.

This implied that Sheriff Gow had not been convinced by witnesses who claimed to have seen 'Stephen' after the separation from his relatives – the barmaid who said she saw him resisting the attentions of a scruffy-looking man in his late forties who carried him struggling out of the Galaxy building; and the motorist who saw a man in a waxed jacket climbing a road into the Garrick Hills hand-in-hand with a young boy. While stressing that he was not criticizing such witnesses, he expressed a preference for the evidence of Mrs Margaret Park, who said she had a clear view of a young boy she later identified as Stephen, gazing – alone – through her caravan window near the camp perimeter fence.

The sheriff also accepted the conclusion of Dr Nancy Cunningham, a consultant pathologist, who was convinced that death had been caused by exposure. 'We can't rule out strangulation,' she said, 'but we can say there was no evidence of ligature marks on the back of the neck which [because of decomposition] was the only part open to us.'

Index